PRAISE FOR DHARMA ROAD

"When I came back from the monastery, I drove a cab for Checker in Boston and can tell you this is the real deal: good taxi and straight dharma."

—Jack Kornfield, author of *A Path with Heart* and *After the Ecstasy, the Laundry*

"This book is wise and witty and direct: very Zen. Also, fun to read."

—Sylvia Boorstein, author of *Happiness Is an Inside Job* and *It's Easier Than You Think: The Buddhist Way to Happiness*

"In *Dharma Road,* Haycock has achieved that rare balance of humor and wisdom. His sense of Buddhism runs deep, born out of his own fascinating experience as a taxi driver. Haycock, the Buddhist cabbie, can take you where you want to go, but more importantly he can take you to the most important landmarks of the dharma. The characters he encounters and the insights he uncovers are well worth the modest fare. His experience demonstrates the Buddhist idea that wisdom doesn't need a temple to live in but manifests in every sort of reflective life."

—Stephen Asma, author of *Why I Am a Buddhist*

"With wry humor and unflinching honesty, Brian Haycock steers the reader through the ups and downs of modern life with the teachings of the Buddha as his road map. An engaging, no-frills introduction to Zen, the dharma, and just sitting at the wheel."

—Stephen Batchelor, author of *Confession of a Buddhist Atheist*

"Compassionate and entertaining . . . and the flow of anecdotes keeps one turning the pages. It is informative about Zen practice, but more importantly the very human insight it gives into one profession—that of cab-driving—illustrates the quality of ordinary compassion that is the hallmark of fully digested Buddhist understanding."

—David Brazier (Dharmavidya),
author of *The Feeling Buddha*

"If the point of life is the journey, travel it via *Dharma Road*. It's accessible, amusing, and wise, with a few surprising forks along the way."

—Arthur Jeon, author of *City Dharma* and *Sex, Love, and Dharma: Finding Love Without Losing Your Way*

"Zen Buddhism comes down from the mountain and hits the streets with Brian Haycock. This gritty, wise, and at times humorous tale shows why Buddhism is exactly what we need in the 21st century. It's practical Buddhism at its finest. You'll enjoy the ride."

—Zan Gaudioso, author of *The Buddha Next Door*

"Wherever you want to go, from wherever you are starting, take a ride in Brian's cab—please, for your sake. The ride will be just grand! His is an honest and down-to-earth voice that has the ring of a good and wise friend, one who has a deep understanding of Zen . . . and human nature."

—David Kundtz, author of *Awakened Mind: One-Minute Wake Up Calls*

DHARMA ROAD

A SHORT CAB RIDE
TO SELF-DISCOVERY

BRIAN HAYCOCK

HAMPTON ROADS
PUBLISHING COMPANY, INC.

Cover design by Hugh D'Andrade

Hampton Roads Publishing Company, Inc.
Charlottesville, VA 22906
www.hrpub.com

Library of Congress Cataloging-in-Publication Data
is available on request.

ISBN: 978-1-57174-635-1
TCP
10 9 8 7 6 5 4 3 2 1
Printed on acid-free paper in Canada

CONTENTS

Introduction: Driving with a Mind Wide Open........ ix

1. Start Your Engines 1

2. This Suffering World 7

3. Craving Attachment 13

4. The Eightfold Freeway..19

5. The Mind of the Rookie 27

6. I Got Attitude.. 35

7. The Cabdrivers' Maintenance Plan 43

8. Attention, Attention, Attention 53

9. Sitting, Not Thinking 63

10. Stop and Smell the Hot Java................................71

11. Get a Grip 79

12. Ac-Ac-Ac-Ac 87

13. Crosstown Traffic..91

14. What I Like 95

15. Clean-Up Time..101

16. Fishing the Moonlight...107

17. Blue Monday...113

18. Thank You, Thank You 119

19. The Right Life 125

20. Loving Loving-kindness......................................133

21. Listen to This 141

22. On the Road to Road Rage 147

23. Let's Fuck with the Cabdriver 153

24. Not Much to Fear 159

25. The Sangha Gang 167

26. In the Shallow End 171

27. A Drive Down Party Lane 177

28. Karma for Kabbies 185

29. The End of the Road 191

30. Metaphysical Me 199

31. Maps and Words 205

32. God Hides in the Traffic 211

33. The Lights Come On (Or at Least Blink) 217

34. New Year's Eve 225

Conclusion: Farther Down the Road 231

Appendix: Airport Reading 235

Dharma Road is dedicated
to cabdrivers and bodhisattvas everywhere.

DRIVING WITH A MIND WIDE OPEN

"Hi. Where would you like to go?"

That's what I always say to people when they get in the cab. It's a friendly greeting that breaks the ice and gets things going on the right foot. I smile when I say it, and I turn partway around, make a little eye contact.

It's a good question. Where do you want to go? Barton Springs for a nice, cool swim? Out to the Oasis to watch the sun go down over Lake Travis? Downtown, maybe to a club on 6th Street to hear some of that good Texas music we like so much here in Austin?

How about a journey of self-discovery? A ride down Dharma Road?

Tuesday afternoon I'm working downtown, checking the hotel stands, cruising the streets. Cab 119, ready to go. I load a woman at the Four Seasons, take her up to the capitol, then take two men from the Omni to the Doubletree. I take a radio call at Brackenridge Hospital and load an old man with a broken leg in a hard cast. He's headed home to an apartment on East 5th, riding on a hospital voucher. He needs a lot of help getting inside. Then I'm back downtown, loading at the Hilton, taking a woman in a gaudy green pantsuit up to the university, listening to her talk about how much she likes Austin, and saying, "Yes, ma'am, I like it here too."

It's a typical afternoon in the cab business. It's a lot like yesterday afternoon. Or tomorrow. It's a lot like your life. There's always something going on, but in the end you wind up pretty much where you started.

Then again, it's not typical at all. It's unique. It's a completely new day, one that will go by and never return. The people, the traffic, the sound and feel of the city. The way everything moves. It's all new, and it will never be this way again. It's all in how you look at it.

Cruising down Congress Avenue, I hear a whistle, see a man wave at me from across the street. I'm all over it. I make a tight U-turn and coast up to the curb in a New York nanosecond. Smooth. Three men in matching dark gray suits going to an office building north on the interstate. One of the men sits in front. He acts a little nervous, fidgety, like there's an important meeting coming up and he's spent the day drinking coffee to get ready for it. He's ready now.

On the seat next to me there's a well-used copy of Seung Sahn's classic *The Compass of Zen*. It's sitting on top of the pile of maps and guidebooks and the clipboard I use to keep track of my cab company paperwork. He picks it up, stares at the cover. "You reading this?" he asks.

"Yeah. It's something to keep me occupied on those long waits at the airport."

"You really understand that Zen shit? It's pretty strange stuff, all that one-hand-clapping shit. That's Zen, right?"

"Yeah, it is. It's a *koan,* a puzzle."

"And you get that?"

"Well, not that, no. Koans are pretty advanced, more for full-time monks. People with the time to put into it. You can't really do that if you're driving a cab ninety hours a week. But Zen's not as confusing as people think. Most of it's just an appreciation for everyday life. The basics are pretty straightforward—there's some philosophy, meditation practice, ethics, that kind of thing. And then you can go on from there, build on that."

He grunts, already losing interest, leans back over the seat, and jumps into a conversation about amortization depreciation allowance something or other, a topic that makes as much sense to me as the one hand clapping does to any of them.

When they get out, he hands me a twenty and says with a grin, "Good luck with that Zen shit." Then he turns and trips over the curb, losing his briefcase as he throws his hands out to catch himself. The case pops open, and papers spill out across the stones.

That's Zen, right there. That moment, the one you didn't expect. The moment when you notice that your life is one little surprise after another. The moment when you realize that ordinary life isn't ordinary at all.

Then again, maybe he shouldn't have called it "Zen shit." That couldn't have been good for his karma.

Welcome to Dharma Road. It'll be a fun ride. Think of it as an introduction to Zen practice for people who live in the real world. People like us. We'll go over the basic ideas of the dharma—the teachings of the Buddha and the others who have followed in his path. We'll talk about morals, meditation, mindfulness. Just the fundamentals. And we'll get started on the day-to-day practice of Zen. This can be pretty serious stuff, but it doesn't have to be. We'll take it easy, make it as clear and concise as possible. And we'll take it out on the streets, see how Zen practice applies in everyday life. We'll try to have a little fun, a few laughs. Because if you're going to put in a sixteen-hour shift behind the wheel, you'll need to have a sense of humor. Maybe we'll even figure out how to make a few dollars along the way. Just like the cabdrivers do. And after that we'll sit back, do a little speculating about what it all means. It'll be quite a ride.

People think of Zen as mystical, inscrutable. Pretty strange. But the basic idea behind Zen is simple: We experience the world through a filter of expectations and preconceptions built up over the course of our lives. As a result, we fail to see the world as it really is. With the help of a program of morality, meditation, and mindfulness, we can overcome this veil of delusion and see through to our own true nature. We can learn to see the world directly and to understand our own place in it.

Simple, isn't it?

It's simple if you only read about it, but in the end you'll have to do more than that. Zen isn't something to read about, it's a way to live. To really understand what's going on here, you'll have to take it into your life and see where it leads you. All I can do is show you the road, fill you in on a few of the moves. The rest is up to you.

Don't worry too much about the cabdriving. You don't have to learn all the streets. Maybe you've already got a career. You may be a doctor, a lawyer, an Internet billionaire. Maybe you're a secret agent battling to prevent a vast ultra-conspiracy from achieving total world domination. Maybe you've put too much into your career to throw it away for this. That's all right. We can't all be cabdrivers. You'll see that life on the streets isn't so different from your life. We all have stress, distractions, delusions. We all get lost sometimes. And we can find ourselves if we try.

So here we go, off on an epic journey of everyday discovery. A sightseeing trip for the soul. Don't forget to buckle up.

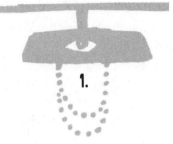

START YOUR ENGINES

Every journey has to start somewhere. For most people taking up a spiritual practice, the starting point is a personal crisis of some kind. It doesn't have to be something dramatic. We're simply unhappy with the way things are and we want to try a different way of living. So we find a new job, a new girlfriend, move to another city. Or we look into a spiritual practice.

If things are going well and we're happy with our lives, we probably won't want to change anything.

It was like that for me. I'd quit drinking, cut way back on some other things. I thought my life would change for the better, and in some ways it did, but I just felt empty. Getting rid of bad habits wasn't enough for me. I had to replace them with something better. So I signed up for an adult education course: Introduction to Zen Buddhism. It could have been Santeria or Channeling Your Inner Space Alien. I didn't put a lot of research into it. I got lucky. A very nice woman taught the course at her suburban home, with meditation practice in her basement *zendo*. She was a great teacher, and the class immediately became the high point of my week. It was a perfect way to get started.

Buddhist history is filled with stories of Zen masters who forced their disciples to wait by the gates of the temple for years to show their determination before they could begin practice. One disciple is said to have cut off his arm and presented it to the master to gain admission. They don't do that now. In major cities, people can walk into a Zen center, get some basic instruction, and start attending functions. Usually there's not much training. Maybe a brief lecture, some instructions on *zazen*, the Zen style of meditation. Then the newcomers join the activities and figure it out as they go along. Outside the cities, people with an interest in Zen might form their own zendo and help each other to learn. Others just buy a few books and a cushion to sit on and start out on their own. In the end, it doesn't really matter. You get out of it what you put in. No matter where you start, it's up to you to make it work.

It's the same with cabdriving. You're on your own, and you can do what you want. You can sit at the airport and wait for the money to roll in, and when it doesn't you can blame the company for not training you well enough. Then you can give up. But if you make the effort, it can work out well for you even without any real training. And you might have a good time doing it. It's not how you start—it's how you proceed.

Cabdrivers usually start out when things are going wrong. Most of them show up at the cab company as a last resort after other things have fallen through. No one writes *cabdriving* in their high school yearbook next to *career path.* They just need a job, any job, to see them through until something better comes along.

That was how I started. I'd worked for an environmental organization for a number of years only to find myself unemployed, broke, and without any real prospects. I knew I'd face some very hard times if I didn't come up with something fast. There was an ad in the paper. I didn't really put a lot of research into it. I went in. I got lucky. Two days later, I was a trainee. That's right, a cabdriver trainee. I was so proud.

The company training program goes on for hours, but most of it is just common sense. The cab business is pretty simple. People get in the cab, tell you where they're going. You drive them there, they pay what the meter says (plus a nice tip), and get out. Then it starts all over again. There's a dispatcher on the radio, putting out calls using a simple set of procedures. You can take calls, letting the calls lead you around. You can sit in cabstands at hotels and restaurants or in a long line at the airport. You can cruise around downtown, see what happens there. You can work the late-night business, covering the clubs downtown. And you can watch the veteran drivers, see how they do things, learn what you can from them.

In Austin, some drivers own their own cabs and pay a weekly fee to one of the companies to cover insurance, permits, and dispatch service. Other drivers lease their cabs. Between the payments and the cost of gas, it can cost a driver more than a hundred dollars a day to stay on the road. That's not easy to make up. A lot of drivers wind up falling behind on their payments and find themselves out of the business. You have to stay focused, and you have to put in the hours. The company training program doesn't really dwell on any of this. If the rookie drivers knew what was coming, they'd probably make a run for it while they could.

Something good about the cab industry: since the drivers are paying the company, rather than the other way around, it's fairly hard to get fired. It happens, but you have to really mess up. In one of the Austin cabdriving legends, a driver managed to run over a passenger who'd gotten out of his cab. Then he drove away. He got fired, but it took the company a week to make the decision.

That story may or may not be true. No one really knows. There are a lot of stories around, and some of them must be true. The streets are paved with urban legends. But the point is, if you've driven a cab, you know: it could happen. It's a pretty strange business.

But then, most businesses are pretty strange. Once you get inside and see what really goes on, you wonder how anything useful ever gets done. Everywhere I've worked I've seen colossal screw-ups, gross incompetence, and outright larceny. Everyone laughs about it over an after-work beer, and nothing ever seems to really change. If you've ever had a job, you know: the working world is a circus. And the clowns are running the show.

Here's another cabdriving story: One night a driver got a package delivery from the airport going to a hospital. It was a cooler, like you'd use for beer. It was kind of a long drive, and he was tired, so he stopped off at home, figuring he'd get some sleep and finish the trip in the morning. After all, it was just a package. You guessed it. There was an organ in the cooler. The cab company had to send another driver to wake him up, collect the cooler, and bring it to the hospital. This sounds crazy, but I'm pretty sure this one actually happened. (No, it wasn't me, and hey, thanks a lot for thinking that.)

For my training, I watched a fifteen-minute video on the proper way to deal with customers. It starred a cab-driver who was polite past the point of being annoying. He looked like a dorky Richard Pryor character from an old movie. He was actually wearing a tie. Then I went out with a veteran driver to spend part of a shift on the streets with him, learning the ropes. He laid rubber getting out of the cab lot.

And he wasn't wearing a tie.

Of course, out here on Dharma Road, we're not really focused on making money. And we're not worried about the inner workings of the cab industry. It doesn't really matter what kind of work we're doing. Most of us are putting a huge chunk of our lives into our jobs, so we'd better get something out of them besides a paycheck. On Dharma Road, we're in this for spiritual growth. Development. Enlightenment, even. We're here to learn something about the way our lives move along these streets, how to make them move more smoothly. How to make them lead somewhere.

We're here to experience our true nature.

Okay, that's enough of the driver training. Now let's get to work.

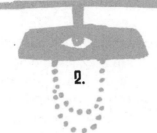

THIS SUFFERING WORLD

It's around noon on a Tuesday. I take a call at an AIDS clinic in a strip mall near the interstate. It's a place for patients without insurance. There's a black woman standing under the awning out of the sun. She looks about thirty, but it's hard to be sure. She's thin—too thin for this life—and she's crying. I pull up, she gets in the back. It takes her three tries to tell me where she's going. "St. David's," she finally tells me, then she starts crying again. St. David's Hospital.

It's a short trip. A half mile. A few minutes. When I pull up at the entrance, she hands me a tear-stained cab voucher. I wish her good luck, but I don't think her luck is going to change that much. I watch her walk in through the sliding glass doors, maybe for the last time. She stops in the lobby and stands there a moment, looking lost.

For the next few hours, I work the streets, thinking about the woman and what she must be going through. Being admitted to the hospital. Going through tests. Seeing the sadness on the faces of the nurses when they look at her. She's scared. Maybe she's alone. Maybe she'll die that way.

The afternoon wears on. It's hot and getting hotter. I'm sitting third in the cabstand outside the Omni, drinking bitter, lukewarm coffee from a Styrofoam cup. I'm thinking about the way my life is going—I'm struggling to make rent, let alone save enough to make a way out of the cab business to something better. I haven't been sleeping well, and I have trouble getting up when I have to. I've got a molar starting to act up and an ache in my lower back from trying to wrestle a hundred-pound suitcase into the trunk. If everything goes well today, I'll be out here tomorrow, doing it all over again. If anything goes wrong, I might not be here at all.

This is my life now: ninety hours a week in a cab, hustling fares, fighting traffic. It wasn't supposed to be this way. My life was going to mean something. I was going to make a difference. I was going to save the world from itself. It didn't happen.

Maybe you had a dream like that. Maybe yours didn't come true either.

"Life is suffering," the Buddha said, and he wasn't kidding around. It's not the uplifting, cheery message you'd expect from the man you see in the statues, the chubby guy with the serene smile and kind eyes. Life is suffering. That was the Buddha's original insight, the one that led him to develop a system of morals and ethics, a program of transformative psychology and a set of guidelines for deep spiritual development.

Everything begins with suffering.

The Buddha was born a prince in a small Indian kingdom. For his first twenty-nine years, he was protected from the harsh realities of life by his doting father. He stayed mostly on the palace grounds, living in luxury, his every desire fulfilled. But he knew there was more to life than simple indulgence. When he finally left the palace and saw the real world for the first time, he was shocked to see the way the common people lived, the hardships that filled their lives. He saw a beggar, a sick person, an old man, and a corpse. Just seeing them changed his life. Poverty, sickness, old age, and death. He was determined to understand why there was so much suffering in life and to learn how it could be overcome. He abandoned his life of privilege and became a wandering monk. Everything in the Buddha's teachings, everything he learned about the human condition, began with that original quest.

I'm watching four young men stand around as a bellman loads their golf bags into the back end of a white stretch limo. They're looking good, wearing their Ban-Lon shirts and their Ray-Ban shades, tanned and fit and more or less rich, heading out to some country club for a round of golf, drinks, some dinner, whatever they want. They don't look like they're suffering all that much.

Maybe they don't need to know about the Buddha's search for understanding. Not today, at least.

But it won't always be this way. During their lives, trouble will find them. It won't all be stretch limos and drinks at the country club, prime ribs on the patio. Today could be the high-water mark of their lives, the day they'll always remember, the one they'll wish they could go back to. Tomorrow it could all go wrong, and they could be left shattered by the loss of what they once had. It can happen.

For most of us, there won't be a spectacular fall. Life is more subtle than that. For most people, life is a mixture of good times and bad. And the better the good times are, the harder the hard times seem. The people who have the easiest lives just get spoiled. They never learn how to cope. They don't think they'll ever have to. Think of Britney Spears going off on a crying jag because her little accessory dog crapped on her $10,000 gown. Or Paris Hilton crying for her mother as she took that limo ride to her week in jail. She could use a couple weeks in Darfur to gain some perspective. Or she could try driving a cab for a while, just to see.

Psychologists have studied happiness as a social and cultural phenomenon. Surprisingly, they've found that people today are no happier than they were a hundred years ago, or two hundred years ago, or at any other time in recorded history. Rates of depression are up, and there's no end in sight. All the material progress that's been made hasn't translated into real happiness. And the rich aren't much happier than other people. Outside of the truly destitute, there is very little correlation between wealth and happiness. The cabdrivers are about as happy as the trust fund kids riding out to the club for a day of golf. They just have different things to complain about. And to appreciate.

Consider Elvis. Once he was the king of the world. He was the King. If anyone should have been able to avoid suffering, it would have been Elvis. He had everything he could ever want, and if he ever saw something else he wanted, he could have had that just by pointing to it. And yet his life turned into an ordeal of emptiness and sorrow, ending in a drug overdose that killed him while he sat on a toilet. If Elvis couldn't achieve real happiness in this life, is there hope for any of us?

Sometimes when I get home, I turn on the TV to help me unwind, and I watch a few minutes of one of those celebrity shows that cover the tragic lives of the icons of our culture. (What can I say? I get home at three in the morning and I don't have cable.) It's a litany of DUIs, eating disorders, and secret heartbreaks. The storybook weddings all seem to end in bitter divorce. How many of the most fortunate wind up in jail, rehab, or both? Too many to count. Or even care about.

And those are the rich and famous people, the ones who've made it big. The celebrities. In a culture obsessed with celebrity, even the celebrities suffer. And so does everyone else, just not in the glare of the spotlights. Take a walk through your local supermarket or down your own Main Street and have a good look at the people you see. Are they happy? Are they satisfied with their lives? Are you?

That's not to say that life is nothing but suffering. Of course it isn't. There are some great ups and crushing downs and a lot of in-betweens. Life is long, and some of it's a lot of fun. But some of it's hard to take. Or it's short, and that's even harder. Like Jim Morrison said, "The future's uncertain and the end is always near." He was right. He turned to heroin to ease his pain, and he died after a few years in the spotlight and a slow slide into darkness.

Out on the streets in a cab, you see plenty of suffering. You meet elderly passengers, some of them fading away, some of them already gone. There are sad and hopeless drunks stumbling around, telling their troubles to the cabdriver after the bartender stops listening. There are crackheads out at four in the morning, hoping to score. There are patients going home from the hospital, heading to clinics for treatment, moving from there to the hospital to die. People who know their lives are running out. Some days, living in this world can just break your heart.

Depressed yet? Don't be. There's a road that leads through the suffering. A road that rises above. We're coming to it.

The guys at the Omni are in the limo now, pulling out, headed for the golf course. Maybe it won't rain out there today. Maybe they'll have a great game and cap it off with a perfectly done surf-and-turf dinner in the clubhouse. Maybe their lives will go on this way forever, free of suffering. I really hope so. But I doubt it. Instead of going out to the course today, they could be setting out with us on a journey of self-discovery. They could be learning about their true nature and learning to rise above the sorrows of life. They could all be buddhas someday.

Maybe they'll get started on that tomorrow.

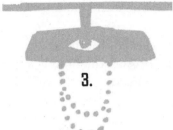

CRAVING ATTACHMENT

I'm driving back from San Marcos with a fifty-dollar bill in my pocket, feeling pretty good. The sun's out, but it's not blasting away. I've got the radio on, an old Johnny Cash road song going. I've been to Buda, Marble Falls, Pflugerville, Cedar Park. . . . I'm thinking I'll work some calls from the radio when I get close to Austin, then try to get something going downtown, maybe make a big day out of it. For a cabdriver, this is heaven.

A 'Vette flashes by on my left, doing eighty. It's silver, lean and hard, and it's just eating up the highway. I can picture the guy inside, in his leather bucket seat, listening to the surround sound, or whatever sound they have in 'Vettes, watching the highway flow on by. I wish I had a 'Vette.

I'm thinking he must have a radar detector. No one does eighty out here without one. I've been thinking about picking one up, but the cab company doesn't really like to see them in the cabs. Besides, it's not in the budget. I pick up the speed a little, watching the back of the 'Vette pull away up the road, watching for his tail-lights.

I wish I had a radar detector. But I won't be buying one anytime soon. And I definitely won't be buying a 'Vette on what I'm making in the cab. Or on anything I can even imagine myself making doing something else. That fifty-dollar fare to San Marcos doesn't seem like such a big deal now. Most of it'll be gone as soon as I stop at a gas station to top off the tank.

I'm not feeling so good now.

The Buddha taught that we suffer because we crave what we cannot have. Whatever we have, we always want more. We're never satisfied. There's always something else, something that would make our lives just right if we could only have it. It just eats at us until we get it. And then we lose interest in that and go on to wanting something else. It just goes on and on, and it seems like there's no way out. The guy in the 'Vette probably wants a Ferrari. Or an airplane. And he's no happier with his 'Vette than I am with this cab.

I'd like a Rolls Royce with the cab package, a fast meter, and a never-ending gas card, but I probably won't get that. I'd also like to date Jennifer Aniston, climb Mount Everest, and discover a cure for cancer. It's not going to happen. Not for me. Not this time around.

People wonder about Elvis, how it could have gone so wrong. I think I understand. It was harder for him. Most of us think we'd be happy if we only had a little more money, a better car, a prettier girlfriend. And we keep trying. At the end, Elvis knew none of that could save him. With all he had, he was still empty. He was as destitute as a crackhead curled up in an alley with his teeth grinding down. He wanted something he couldn't have, something he couldn't even name. And he knew he'd never have it. It wasn't the pills that killed him. It was the emptiness. The pills only finished him off.

More than anything, we fear losing what we already have. We become attached to the things in our lives that bring us pleasure, but those things are only temporary. Fleeting. So we hold on, tighter and tighter, but that doesn't work. Everything is changing, all the time, and all our attachments will be broken in the end. The rock-and-rollers will lose their edge, their records will stop selling, and they'll be doing nostalgia tours, wondering where it all went. The beauties will lose their looks, the athletes will slow down. Change is the only constant. Nothing lasts forever. You can't go home again, no matter where you're from.

Most of the changes in our lives are slow and subtle. We don't even notice them. But they add up.

Driving around Austin, you get a sense of constant change in the landscape. There are construction cranes and wrecking balls everywhere you look. It seems like they've always been there. Living here for over twenty years, I feel like I've moved to another city, a little at a time.

When I first moved to Austin, there was a place near where I lived called Beer Park. That's right, Beer Park. This is Texas—people think like that here. There were picnic tables set up, a horseshoe pit, a makeshift stage. Sometimes there were people playing guitars, just kicking it around, having fun. I'd go there after work with some of my friends, have a roast beef sandwich, a glass of beer. It lasted six months. The University of Texas bought the land, tore everything down, and built a maintenance facility on it.

Our lives change more quickly and surely than any landscape. Friends drift off, move away. We move, change jobs, join clubs, take up causes, lose interest in them, fall in and out of love. It's not always a bad thing: we all want some variety, some change to make things interesting. Some of the changes are for the better, some for the worse. But very little in life lasts for long. And nothing lasts forever.

According to the Buddha, the events of our lives have no independent existence. They are only temporary. It's all a house of cards. Everything arises and fades away. Ashes to ashes, all fall down. This is a world of shadow and light, nothing more than a show. It's fun to watch, but that's about all.

The suffering we feel isn't caused by the fact of impermanence itself. Impermanence isn't good or bad, it's just the way things are. It's like gravity, or gas prices or the long cab lines at the airport. The problem is our habit of craving what we cannot have and becoming attached to things that cannot last. Then, when they're gone, we feel the loss.

I've gotten attached to the cab I drive, number 119. It's an ex-police car with a big V-8, heavy-duty brakes and suspension, about as well built as a car can be. I spend more time in the cab than I spend at home. A lot more. I've driven so many miles in it, I feel like it's an extension of myself, a suit of clothes I put on in the morning. Sometimes it goes in for service and I have to spend an afternoon in another car. I feel uncomfortable, awkward. Everything just feels wrong, and I can't wait to get back in my regular cab. But 119 has over 200,000 miles on it and there's a vibration in the transmission that shouldn't be there. It won't last forever.

When the cab goes down, I'll move on to a new one, and I'll get used to that and I'll probably get attached to it. It's all right. I've got some perspective on it. It's only a car, after all. But when we form strong attachments to things in our lives that cannot last, they lead to suffering in the end. Like anyone, I look back at some of the good times I've had, and I wish I could go back, live that way again. But I can't.

In Buddhism, four sources of suffering are unavoidable: birth, sickness, old age, and death. Birth and the process of growing up are painful, both physically and emotionally. Sickness, old age, and death are great sources of suffering for most people, but the real problem is only our reactions to these changes in our lives.

Life begins in suffering. We are pushed from the warmth and safety of the womb to find ourselves in an uncertain and dangerous world, gasping for breath. The first thing we do is cry. It's a good thing we can't remember our birth. We'd be traumatized.

Old age can only be avoided by dying, so old age is really a good thing. The elderly are fortunate to have lived so long. But it's hard to think of it that way. They have aches and pains and can't do the things they used to do. Old age is hard because we're so attached to our youth. We remember the things we could do then, how good it felt to be young and strong, how fresh and new the world seemed. And we miss that.

We're attached to our good health while we have it, so when we're sick, we suffer from more than just our symptoms. Some people have had health problems for years, and they've gotten used to a certain amount of sickness in their lives. It doesn't seem to bother them as much. People who have been fortunate enough to enjoy good health for most of their lives are in for a shock when they get sick. I get a cold every few years, and that's about it. So far. When I get a cold, I'm the most miserable person on earth. I'm pathetic. I just whine and complain until it goes away. My time will come: I'll get really sick, and I won't be able to handle it at all. That's how attachment works.

And then there's death. We all know it's coming, so it should be easy to accept, but it isn't. We're attached to our lives and want them to go on forever. But they don't, and people who have to face death are truly filled with suffering. Even if they don't let it show.

When the Buddha began to teach, he was asked what his teaching consisted of. He said, "I teach suffering and the end of suffering." Now, after twenty-five hundred years, the Buddha is still teaching the end of suffering. He's teaching it to us.

The way to end our suffering is to let go of our cravings, to give up our attachments to the impermanent events of our lives. If we can learn to accept the temporary nature of all things, to see them simply as events to be appreciated for themselves without trying to hold on to them, then we can live without suffering. That is the basis of Buddhist practice, the entry to the Eightfold Path, the blueprint for a life free of suffering.

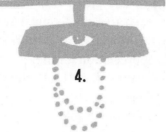

THE EIGHTFOLD FREEWAY

In everything we do, we need guidance. Direction. I've got a stack of map books, tourist guides, and a pocket edition of the Yellow Pages next to me on the front seat so I can find my way around town. Anywhere I need to go, I can find my way. In life, it's harder. There's no set of map books for day-to-day living. Every day, we have to make important, sometimes critical, decisions. There are always intersections, choices to be made. Like Yogi Berra said, "When you come to a fork in the road, take it." There are a lot of forks. And, being human, we're not that good at figuring them out. We need a guide to help us through. Help is available. In Buddhism, the basic guide for spiritual practice is called the Eightfold Path.

Being a cabdriver, I think of the Eightfold Path as a road map for the soul. A spiritual OnStar. Using another metaphor, Korean Zen master Seung Sahn describes it as "having eight different medicines for each of the mind's sicknesses." Road map or medicine; cabdriver, Zen master, or mental patient; the Eightfold Path defines the day-to-day practice of Buddhism. And it defines an approach to daily living that simply works, whether the goal is spiritual realization, peace of mind, or just a simple appreciation for life.

The Buddha's original teaching, the teaching about suffering and the end of suffering we saw in the last chapter, is known as the Four Noble Truths. The First Noble Truth is simply that suffering is a fundamental part of the human condition. The second is that suffering is the result of our cravings and our attachment to things and events in our lives that are impermanent. The Third Noble Truth is that there is a solution to the problem of suffering. The fourth is the practice that can lead to the end of suffering. That practice is the Eightfold Path.

The Four Noble Truths follow an ancient Indian logical form. First, a problem is stated, then the cause of the problem, then whether or not a solution exists, and then the solution. It's a diagnosis and treatment plan for the human condition.

Much of the dharma is presented in the form of lists. There was no written language in ancient India, so Buddhism began as an oral tradition. Lists are a great aid for memory, and they were used to express everything. There are the Three Jewels, the Ten Grave Precepts, the Five Skandhas, the Six (or Ten) Paramitas, the Twelve Links in the Chain of Dependent Origination. Somewhere in the dharma, there is probably a list of Seventeen Really Important Lists. The lists can seem tedious, but they help to organize a number of difficult ideas into a comprehensible form. And the lists themselves can be organized into a framework. The Four Noble Truths lead to the Eightfold Path, and steps on the Eightfold

Path lead to other aspects of the practice, many of them given as more lists.

The Four Noble Truths are the origin of Buddhism. The Eightfold Path is the actual practice, the road to understanding. Taken together, the steps on the path describe a life dedicated to spiritual growth and development. The steps of the Eightfold Path are:

1. Right view
2. Right thought
3. Right speech
4. Right action
5. Right livelihood
6. Right effort
7. Right mindfulness
8. Right meditation

The first two steps on the Eightfold Path are often referred to as the wisdom steps. The first step, right view or right understanding, is to learn about the philosophies and practices of Buddhism and to see how they apply in everyday life. We can do this by reading, by attending lectures and dharma events, and just by living in this world and seeing how things go together. Reading *Dharma Road* is a small, tentative start on this first step. Developing a right view also means not being limited by our own preconceptions or, in the words of Seung Sahn, "having no view." We all have our own points of view, and we interpret new ideas in terms of our past experiences. Part of the first step is to put aside our concepts and study the dharma with fresh eyes and a clear mind.

The second step, right thought, is also known as right intention. This means to use wisdom to attain true enlightenment for the benefit of all beings, not for any kind of personal gain. It also means to avoid attachment to our own opinions and to avoid self-deceptions of all kinds. Taken together, the first two steps on the path give a clear sense of the importance of gaining wisdom without becoming attached to it.

The next three steps, right speech, right action, and right livelihood, relate to living ethically. Ethics are important in Buddhist practice partly because spiritual practice depends on having a clear conscience. You can't move ahead while you're looking over your shoulder, worrying about the things you've done. And wondering when they'll come back to haunt you. Following these steps on the path helps avoid inner conflicts and the ruined karma they can cause.

The basic idea of right speech is to use our words to express ourselves as we want to be. That is, to speak as a buddha would speak. This means to use our words to help others, not only to help ourselves. It means using our words constructively, avoiding gossip, harsh language, and other self-centered speech. It also means to tell the truth, avoiding not only outright lies, but also exaggerations and half-truths.

And it means not to yell out the window at the amateur drivers. A buddha wouldn't speak like that.

Living our day-to-day lives in a moral and ethical manner is called right action. This is a very general step, one that is developed in greater detail in the various schools of Buddhism. It simply means to act mindfully and constructively. Right action leads to practices of compassion such as loving-kindness and the *bodhisattva* ideal and to the Ten Grave Precepts, which define moral actions in daily life. Lama Surya Das sums up this step as, "Treating others as you yourself would be treated." Think of it as the Buddhist version of the Golden Rule.

Right livelihood has special meaning for the cabdrivers of the world. Generally, right livelihood means to make a living constructively, without harming others. While we can't all find employment that relates directly to improving the lives of others, we can all make an effort to have a positive effect through the work we do. That means we should try to use our workdays to make the world a better place. And we should use them as a basis for our own spiritual growth.

Given the importance of work in the modern world, right livelihood takes on added significance for all of us. On Dharma Road, we'll be paying extra attention to the ways livelihood and spiritual practice can reinforce each other. And if we can make that happen in a cab, then all you secret agents, movie stars, and Internet billionaires out there can find ways to use your jobs as a basis for personal growth as well.

The last three steps on the Eightfold Path relate to meditation and the development of mindfulness. This is the real spiritual work of Buddhism. Meditation practice is the foundation for personal growth: practicing helps build mindfulness, and with greater mindfulness, the other steps on the path become more natural, easier to take. As we follow the other steps, the meditation practice grows stronger. The Eightfold Path is really meant as a cycle that runs through the steps again and again, in any order at all, with each step reinforcing the others and each cycle strengthening the practice.

Step six, right effort, is to make a consistent effort to develop a strong and effective practice. Buddhist practice is not hard work—there's no heavy lifting—but it takes effort and dedication to stay with it day after day. There are always distractions, excuses for avoiding practice, but these distractions must be overcome for this to develop into something more than a hobby. At first it's hard to make that commitment. It just takes a little faith to believe that the effort will pay off in time.

Right mindfulness means that we should concentrate fully on our everyday activities, not letting our minds wander, not becoming lost in our thoughts. This is the hardest step of all, because it has to be practiced every minute of every day—24/7, you could say. It's hard, but the development of mindfulness is the key to spiritual growth. Seeing the world as it truly is, instead of being caught up in our own small view of it, requires years of practice. Even the most mundane activities can be used as opportunities for spiritual development if approached with an open and active mind. We should take full advantage of them. And we should be mindful of ourselves as well.

The last step is right meditation. Meditation practice is the most important tool for developing mindfulness and making progress toward enlightenment. There are many variations on the basic techniques, and some exploration of them can be helpful. Of course, every school claims that its techniques are right, and the others are, well, less right. In the end, it's up to each of us to develop a meditation practice that works for us. And to stay with it.

The Eightfold Path consists of general guidelines rather than strict rules. Strict rules only get in the way. The idea is to interpret the ideas of the path and apply them in real-life situations. Follow the spirit of the Eightfold Path rather than the letter, and follow it honestly and wholeheartedly. Flexibility is one of the keys to the entire practice. The path is the same for a twenty-first century cabdriver as it was for a tenth-century Tibetan recluse or a third-century BC Indian *arhant*. It's all in the application.

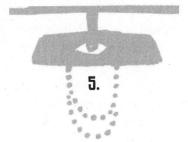

THE MIND OF THE ROOKIE

Whatever we do in life, we have to start somewhere. We're all beginners sometimes. We might be new at the zendo, trying to figure out the rituals, trying not to do anything to embarrass ourselves. We'll figure it out in time, but it's a little awkward at first. Out on the streets, the new cabdrivers are called rookies. They don't really know what they're doing yet. They're driving around lost half the time, confused all the time, trying to learn a job that's turning out to be a lot more difficult than they thought it would be. Some of them are angry about the way it's going, some are feeling overwhelmed. But they're not bored out there. Every shift is an adventure for them, a memorable experience. And when the shift is done, they're thinking it over, figuring out what worked, what didn't work, what they'll do differently next time.

One of the worst things one cabdriver can say about another is to call him a rookie. It means he's incompetent, not fit to be thought of as a real cabdriver. On the radio, you'll hear the dispatcher trying to explain to a new driver how to use the radio codes, or asking him why he hasn't picked up the call he was given a half hour ago. And the veterans are out in their cabs, listening to this, muttering, "Fucking rookies!"

Another name for the rookies is fresh meat. It's a tough business, and there's not that much compassion out there for the new guys.

The veteran cabdrivers love to bitch about the rookies. They also bitch about the dispatchers, the cab company, the traffic, the weather, the passengers. They bitch about each other. They bitch about their own lives and the way they're going. It's a regular bitchfest out there. And the rookies catch more than their share of it.

When I started, I made a real effort to avoid embarrassing myself on the radio. For a while, I worked mostly out of the airport and the hotel cabstands. I worked late downtown, lining up along 6th Street to take the drunks home. I'd take radio calls only when I was sure I could cover them quickly. If I got lost, I'd figure it out without calling in. And through it all, I kept the radio on, listened to what was said, what wasn't said, what set the dispatchers off. It was more important to me to earn the other drivers' respect than to make money right off. And I learned. Before long, I was working the radio on a regular basis without sounding too much like a rookie. The other drivers would ask me how long I'd been driving, and they'd be surprised when I'd say, "I'm just a rookie."

I'm not a rookie now, but I've tried to keep the attitude I started with, the idea that I don't really know that much about what's going on, that I have to pay attention, try to learn all I can. Now when the passengers, making small talk, ask how long I've been driving, I tell them, "Only a few months." Just to stay sharp. And I try to keep my rookie attitude, playing the role of a new driver still excited about his new job. This violates my commitment to right speech, but it's only a little lie, and it helps me remember what it was like being a rookie. Of course, this ruse has a nice side benefit: if I do something really stupid, like making a wrong turn or forgetting to punch the meter, we can put that down to mere inexperience, not utter stupidity.

I don't usually talk about Zen practice when I'm out in the cab, but when people see one of my books on the seat and ask about it, I always tell them I'm just a beginner. It's not to avoid talking about it—which I don't really mind doing—it's because I don't want to turn my practice into something I talk about, part of my persona. I don't want to start pretending to be a Zen master, making a big deal about it. Or about myself. It's supposed to be who I am to myself, not who I am to the world.

There's another practical side to thinking like a rookie. When I started driving a cab, I listened to the veteran drivers talk about their strategies, and I noticed that most of them had figured out what to do when they started out, and then they stuck with it. Times change, and many of them hadn't adapted. One of the worst pieces of advice I ever got was from an older driver who'd been working the streets on and off for almost twenty years. He advised me to avoid working the UT football games. They were too much trouble, he said, and most of the trips were short. The next week, I worked the game and booked a hundred dollars in three hours. Apparently something had changed. Most of the veterans spent those three hours sitting in line at the airport, playing cards, talking about the dumb rookies out working the game. They weren't adapting.

But the real benefit of thinking like a rookie isn't the practical one. Rookies just have a better time, and they get more out of the experience. The veterans get burned out and tired, and they don't enjoy it much at all.

There's a short story by Thomas Wolfe, "Only the Dead Know Brooklyn." The idea behind the title is that Brooklyn is so big, it would take a lifetime to learn it all. Austin's so spread out, it's probably a lot bigger than Brooklyn. I don't know half of it. There are veteran cab-drivers who come close to knowing it all, but they've stopped trying to keep up with it. Knowing everything there is to know sounds like a good thing, even if it's only the layout of a city, but not if it means losing the excitement that comes with new experiences. And a lot of the veteran drivers know everything about cabdriv-ing—or they think they do.

The idea of the beginner's mind in Zen is associ-ated with the late Soto Zen master Shunryu Suzuki. Suzuki-roshi came to this country from Japan in 1958 and founded the San Francisco Zen Center and the Zen Mountain Center. His book, *Zen Mind, Beginner's Mind*, is the inspiration for Soto Zen practice throughout the Western world. It's a collection of his dharma talks, organized into a comprehensive introduction to Zen practice. It was the first book on Zen I ever read, and it's still my favorite.

In his teachings, Suzuki-roshi developed the concept of the beginner's mind—one that is open and alert, not closed in by preconceptions. When we lose that beginner's spirit, we become jaded, inattentive, dull. In one of Suzuki-roshi's examples, he says that reciting a sutra once might be a meaningful practice, but reciting it for the tenth time might be merely a chore. In Zen practice, the five hundredth reading should be as fresh and as meaningful as the first. Otherwise, why do it at all? As Suzuki-roshi put it: "In the beginner's mind there are many possibilities; in the expert's there are few." The aim of Zen practice is to recover the beginner's mind and maintain it in daily life.

Seung Sahn uses a similar concept in his teaching. He emphasizes the "don't-know mind"—a clear, open mind that exists before learning, before knowledge, before opinions. The don't-know mind, like the beginner's mind, is open to experience, free of the preconceptions that keep us from direct perception of reality.

Learning to drive is a good example of what it's like to be a beginner. Like most people, I took driver's ed in high school. It was an important rite of passage for all of us then, and no doubt still is. I learned to drive in an old-style Pontiac, the one with the long wheelbase, the wide-track wheels, the massive chrome bumpers. The car was huge and made completely of heavy steel with a soft suspension system that made it sway like a boat on the turns. A big, almost-out-of-control, top-heavy boat. At my high school, the car was nicknamed Godzilla. Every ride in that car was an epic adventure.

Driver's ed was a tough experience for me. I was sixteen, trying hard not to be nervous but not quite pulling it off. I went out onto the streets after about ten minutes of practice in the school parking lot and struggled just to keep the car on the road. Godzilla would drift to the right, I'd overcompensate, drift to the left. I'd overcompensate again. At stop signs, I'd either put too much pressure on the brakes and lurch to a stop or I'd use too little and roll into the intersection. It would have bothered me, but everyone else did the same thing. Driving that monster was an ordeal for everyone, but great training, since every other car on the road would be a lot easier to drive.

Driver's ed was also great fun. Driving around in Godzilla, I felt completely alive. My senses seemed magnified, my mind full-out alert. I was aware of everything going on around me, the roar of the V-8, the car swaying around the curves, the oncoming traffic, the gasps from the driver's ed teacher, his foot moving toward the passenger-side brake pedal, just in case.

Today, I'm driving an average of two hundred miles a day in a sedan that feels like a 'Vette compared to that hunk of steel. Driving is second nature to me now. I don't really have to think at all to do it, and much of the time, I don't. I'll carry on a conversation with a passenger, listen to the dispatcher on the radio, sip coffee, think about other things. Sometimes, ironically, I think about mindfulness while I'm driving.

It's that way with any activity. At first it's exciting, and it's easy to get caught up in it. But after a while, it's all second nature and it becomes just a chore. Jobs can be like that: at first everything seems new and a little complicated, and you find yourself going over it in your mind at night, figuring it out. After about a month, it's all just a crushing bore and you can't wait to get out of there. I've given up on most of the hobbies I've taken up, just lost interest when I was starting to do a little better at them. Not all of them, but it's been a problem for me. In the long run, it's important to learn from experience, to develop what Buddhists call skillful means in whatever you do, but it's also important to keep that beginner's mind alive, to have a sense of excitement about even the most mundane activities of life.

Like driving. Or cabdriving.

In many fields, the best work is done by people in their twenties. Albert Einstein formulated the theory of relativity when he was twenty-six. All his important work was done before he turned forty. After that, he was unable to adapt to the advent of quantum mechanics. While this is usually attributed to age, another factor is the openness and enthusiasm of the newcomer. The young Einstein was able to see the contradictions of classical physics without the preconceptions that kept other scientists back. The older Einstein interpreted everything that came along in terms of his earlier work, and that was the wrong approach for some of the new problems that came up. For whatever reason, he'd lost his beginner's attitude, his don't-know mind.

This applies to Zen practice itself. At times, it can become boring, just another routine in a life filled with routines. Keeping the practice fresh is one of the greatest challenges we face. It's beaten me more than once. Just when I start to make some real progress, I get bored, dissatisfied, and I start to find excuses to put it off. I'll tell myself I need to be out on the street in the morning and I won't do my zazen. Then at the end of my shift, I'll forget about practice, have a glass of wine to help me fall asleep instead. When this happens, the only way to keep my practice fresh is to attack it with a new enthusiasm, forcing myself to sit diligently morning and night, to keep it in mind during the day.

It takes a lot of effort to be a beginner. And even more to stay one.

I'm out here driving down this Eightfold Freeway, thinking I know a little bit about driving, something about the streets. I've been around the block a few times, so I must have learned a few things on the way. But the truth is, I'm just a rookie cabdriver, nothing more. And nothing less. Sometimes I think I know a little bit about Zen. But I'm really just a rookie at that too. A beginner. Nothing more and nothing less.

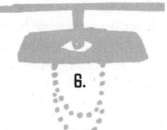

I GOT ATTITUDE

If you're going to drive a cab, there's one thing you'll need to develop right away: an attitude. Hang around with the cabdrivers for a while and you'll hear it. Attitude is everything. You hear that a lot in the cabstands, out at the airport. Driving the long hours, putting up with the traffic, the customers, the other aggravations, drivers have to work to stay positive.

"Attitude is everything," they say. "And I've got one."

What they mean is, watch out for me. I'm tough. You hear the De Niro line from *Taxi Driver* a lot: "Are you talking to me? Are you . . . talking to me? [Dramatic pause.] Well, I'm the only one here." Some of the drivers practice that in the mirror just like Travis Bickle did so they can nail it if it ever comes up.

But that's not the kind of attitude we're trying to develop here.

Actually we've all got attitudes, all the time. We approach everything in life with a set of expectations based on our past experiences. Sometimes those expectations can turn negative and make our lives even more difficult than they need to be. In cabdriving, the results are fast and dramatic. People who expect the worst generally get what they expect, while the optimists get all the breaks. It just seems to go that way. So it's best to start out with a positive attitude.

An essential teaching from Tibetan Buddhism is that we make the world with our minds alone. Our thoughts make our reality. Volumes have been written about the metaphysical implications of this, but we won't be going into that right now. The common sense, everyday version of this teaching is simply that our experience of the world around us is highly subjective. We respond to our impressions of events, and to the values we put on them, not to the reality itself. Those impressions are purely in our minds.

For example, there's Albert Einstein's classic description of relativity. A few seconds touching a hot stove seems like a long time. Ten minutes talking to a pretty girl seems like no time at all. There's more to relativity than this, but the point is that our experience of the world is truly subjective. And relative.

Take the weather. The weather in Central Texas is a constant source of amazement. In the summer, it's a hundred degrees in the shade. It gets so hot in the afternoon that the air conditioners in the cabs can't keep up unless they're parked in the shade. There's no shade in the airport lot. You'll see drivers pouring cold water on their cars to get the heat out, blocking the windows up with cardboard. On a bad day, one of the drivers will stand at the exit from the lot hosing down the cabs as they pull out to go up to the terminal.

When it's clear outside, the sunlight is a lethal bath of ultraviolet radiation. When the winds die, the exhaust fumes pile up, the ozone builds, and the dead, unmoving air just hangs over the city. There are bizarre hazes that blow in from West Texas dust storms, Guatemalan forest fires, and burning tire dumps all over the Southwest. There are droughts that go on for months and end in torrents of rain and flash floods. There are tornadoes strong enough to blow entire towns into piles of rubble.

It's also the allergy capital of the United States.

We love it.

In August you can sit in front of the airport and watch the people coming in from Chicago, New York, all over. They come out of the terminal, walk about five feet, then start looking around, wondering who put a blast furnace in front of the airport. Walking over to the cabs, they pull off their jackets, loosen their ties. Sweat starts to pop out on their shirts. They don't wait at the back of the car for the driver to stow the luggage in the trunk; they just head straight for the air conditioned back seat.

People from out of town who get in the cab at the airport all ask the same question: "Is it always this hot?"

"Hot? Well, I guess you could call this hot. You should have been here last week. It was really hot then. This isn't so bad." I've just spent two hours in a cab line, all of it outside, and if the heat bothered me that much, I'd have passed out back there. Actually, the problem isn't just the heat, it's also the glacial temperatures on the planes and in the terminal. If they'd tone down the air conditioning, people wouldn't have these problems. But people don't want to hear about that. They want to be told how brave they are for dealing with the conditions.

Living here, you get used to the heat. You acclimate to it. And you catch on to the fact that whining about it just makes it worse. So you take some precautions—drink fluids, stay out of the sun, that kind of thing—and you don't dwell on it.

In Zen terms: don't attach to the weather.

Attitude, they say, is everything. If you let the weather get you, it will. The same goes for other obstacles in life. Whatever you face, whining about it won't help. Do what you can to deal with it, and then let it go. Adapt to conditions and stop wishing conditions would adapt to you. Because the fact is, they won't.

That's attitude.

When I first signed on as a cabdriver, I was sinking fast. I'd had other jobs, jobs I believed in, jobs I enjoyed doing. For a while I thought I was going make a difference in the world, maybe make a decent living doing it. Then a job I'd poured myself into for years turned into a soul-sucking visit to the inner realms of hell. I finally found myself unemployed, with no offers coming in. I was struggling just to stay afloat. I was discouraged, disillusioned. It was a hard time for me, but I knew I had to maintain some hope that things would get better. I knew I had to keep a positive attitude or things would get even worse. The way I felt, it could have gone either way.

That's when I started cabdriving.

Around the end of my first week in the cab, I loaded a family at the airport and took them out to Bastrop, a thirty-dollar fare. That brightened my outlook, but I knew it was just one good fare, nothing more than that.

After I dropped them off, I stopped at a barbecue joint out on the Bastrop Highway, had a brisket plate with all the fixins, which was pretty nice. Real Texas food. On the way back, I found myself enjoying the ride. I was starting to feel comfortable with the car I was driving, a fairly late-model ex-police special that was a lot more fun to drive than the cargo van I'd been slogging around in before. Thinking about it that way, things didn't seem so bad. I felt some of the gloom I'd been feeling for the past few months dropping away.

Coming back into Austin, I crested a hill and found myself driving into a spectacular sunset with the radio set to KGSR, Sandy Denny singing "Who Knows Where the Time Goes?"—a great song about impermanence and loss—and I was overcome by the beauty of the moment. There were tears in my eyes, and my heart felt full for the first time in months. I pulled onto the shoulder and held on to the feeling for as long as I could. Sunsets and great songs aren't rare, but they go by quickly and they're easy to miss. Often we're too caught up in our own concerns to even notice them, and we miss out on the beauty around us.

Of course, if I'd gotten a lousy eight-dollar fare to the Omni, I would have missed out on that moment too. But there would have been other moments. There always are, but you have to be open to them. You have to notice them.

Surviving the summer heat and appreciating those special moments aren't the only reasons to try to keep a positive attitude. Even for a veteran cabdriver, staying positive is a necessity. Cabdriving is a constant source of irritations and aggravations. Try driving a sixteen-hour shift in a state of anger and depression. It won't work out. The only way to persevere is to smile and enjoy the ride, no matter how many ruts there are in the road.

Attitude is important in everyday life, and if you're going to have an attitude, it's best to have a positive one. Those negative attitudes can suck the life right out of you. But in Zen, attitude isn't everything. It's only a step toward something larger. In Zen practice, an attitude is just another distraction. If we want to learn about our true nature, we have to let go of our attitudes. They're only functions of ego and the small, deluded mind. Even a positive attitude keeps us from seeing the world as it truly is and ourselves as we truly are. If we see the world through rose-colored glasses we'll miss out on all the other colors. In the wider view, the hard, ugly moments are just as full as the great songs and the glorious sunsets. It's hard to see that sometimes, but it's true.

That's one of the great things about cabdriving. There are plenty of hard, ugly moments to appreciate.

Meditation and mindfulness practice are geared toward clearing away the attitudes and preconceptions that affect our perceptions of the world around us. The mind of a buddha doesn't have any attitude at all: it's just a mirror of the world. To a buddha, the potholes are just part of the road, and it doesn't take an attitude adjustment to deal with them. So in Zen practice, we try to keep a positive attitude while whittling away at our need to have any attitude at all.

But we're not buddhas yet. We're just rookies at this. We're trying to learn about ourselves. A good way to get started is just to observe our reactions to the situations—both good and bad—that come up in our lives.

When we catch a run of green lights, we can get excited even though we know that the lights will even out in the long run. When we hit a pothole, we can say, "It's just a pothole." Or we can turn around and yell at the pothole. If we're paying attention, we'll get a good laugh out of most of our reactions. Because, really, they're just green lights and potholes.

THE CABDRIVERS' MAINTENANCE PLAN

The Eightfold Freeway isn't an easy drive. It's a long road, and there are potholes and pitfalls, ordeals to endure, endless distractions to overcome. It takes a real commitment to cover the journey. Most of all, it takes a driver with the strength to stay on the road when the other drivers have given up and turned in their keys. Whether the goal is cosmic enlightenment or just a decent living, the freeway is a marathon. It's not a quick jog down the block.

We're in this for the long run, and we have to be prepared. Maintenance is critical. For ourselves and for our cars.

It's a tough road for a working cab. Even the hardiest taxicabs don't last forever. They take a beating out on the road, running up the mileage and eventually running down. A typical cab will rack up seventy thousand miles in a year. And those are hard miles. Cabdriver miles.

Most of the cabs start out as police cruisers or other fleet vehicles. They're auctioned off when the mileage starts to add up. That's when they get a coat of yellow paint and hit the street for real. By the time a cab is retired from the cab fleet, it's likely to be on its second engine and its third transmission. There should be a graveyard for retired cabs, maybe a rural parking lot with a nice view where they could sit in the sun and rust in peace. There isn't. They just get stripped, crushed, and melted down.

For the cabs, maintenance is critical.

It's not just the cars that wear down. The drivers are putting in the same miles, putting up with the wear and tear of the city streets. Working eighty hours a week or more, week after week, it's easy to break down, crack up, or just run out of gas. The drivers have to be maintained as much as the cabs. Staying healthy is as much a part of cabdriving as working the streets and dealing with the people.

Many cabdrivers are seriously overweight—obese or nearly so. Others are painfully thin, their faces pinched, their eyes haunted, bones sticking out. They're bundles of nerves, always in a hurry, stressed out, never taking enough time to eat a decent meal. But they've got plenty of time for cigarettes. Some of the drivers—mostly the rookies—are in decent shape so far. They haven't been doing this long enough to suffer serious damage. Not yet.

It's not a healthy lifestyle. There's no exercise involved in the job other than lifting an occasional suitcase into the trunk and walking into a 7-Eleven for coffee and a Twinkie. The hours are long, so there's not much time for outside activities. And most of the drivers are eating drive-thru at burger joints or picking up a pizza on the way home, so bad nutrition is a given. They're drinking a lot of coffee to keep them going, and then having trouble sleeping when they go home. Then there's the stress. There's a lot of stress. Add it all up, and it's a prescription for a short, painful life.

Sound familiar? Cabdrivers aren't the only ones headed for trouble. These are national epidemics, and they affect us all.

On the plus side, most cabdrivers don't drink, since they don't have any real time off and drinking in a cab is just not an option. It's the same with drugs. But a lot of the drivers look like they could really use a night off, a belt of bourbon, and a fat joint. And a salad.

The cabdrivers' body types reflect the paths of self-indulgence and asceticism. The Buddha grew up in an atmosphere of self-indulgence, with feasting a steady part of his life. When he set out on his spiritual path, he practiced self-denial, including rigorous fasting. Neither approach brought him peace of mind, and he finally developed the Middle Way, a healthy, constructive path between the destructive extremes he'd previously followed. Of course, diet and exercise are only a small part of the Buddha's way, but they are important. It's hard to accomplish much spiritual development in a diabetic coma.

When I started driving a cab, I was in good shape. I'd been exercising, doing a little running, eating a sensible diet. I saw the other drivers, the shape they were in, and I didn't think it could happen to me. For a while, it didn't. Then I started going downhill. I was eating doughnuts for breakfast and drinking 7-Eleven coffee all day. I'd get a bacon cheeseburger and fries from the Jack in the Box line on the way home and eat it at three in the morning. I wasn't really eating more than usual, but I wasn't working it off either. I suddenly started gaining weight. In a few months, I'd put on twenty pounds, none of it muscle.

That's right, a bacon cheeseburger. This is Texas. This is the state that tried to throw Oprah in jail for bad-mouthing beef. They shoot vegetarians here. At least I think they do. I'm not a vegetarian and if I was, I wouldn't admit it in public. Surprisingly, the Buddha wasn't a vegetarian either. He and his followers begged food from townspeople as they traveled, and they accepted what they were given. And while many Buddhists are vegetarians, it's not required. What is required is to be very aware of the sacrifice made by the animals we eat.

The weight wasn't my only problem. I'd smoked cigarettes my whole adult life, and it hadn't seemed to bother me: now I was smoking more, having one after every fare, getting rattled whenever I ran out. I had headaches and insomnia from the stress of the road. Zen practice should have helped with that, but I was letting that slide a little too. I knew I would be in real trouble if I didn't straighten out right away.

Then one day, the cab I was driving broke down and there weren't any available, so I had to take a few days off. I got a ride downtown from one of the other drivers and walked home from there. It was about two miles, a distance I'd always been able to walk with no trouble. It wore me out. Halfway there, I felt like calling a cab. I had to sit on a bench just to gather myself. When I got home, I spent the rest of the day lying on the couch, recovering from a walk that wouldn't have bothered me at all a few months earlier.

That got my attention. I started an exercise program, working out in the mornings, alternating three sets of exercises, each taking about fifteen minutes. Nothing dramatic, but enough to reverse the spiral I'd fallen into. I cut back on the coffee. I started keeping my cigarettes in the glove compartment, then in the trunk, getting one out only when I really needed one. I cut way down on the pizza, started watching my diet, although I'd still hit the drive-thrus more often than I really should've. And I'd do a little walking when I could, mostly a few laps around the lot out at the airport just to get the blood going, sometimes a jog around a couple of blocks in the morning.

I started feeling better right away. The weight eventually came off, and the muscle tone came back. I cut down on the cigarettes (I've since quit). And I pushed myself harder to keep my Zen practice alive. I scheduled my zazen and stopped making excuses to miss it. That helped with everything else. When you're focused on overcoming delusion and seeing though to your true nature, it's hard to get excited about pizza.

The Buddha is sometimes portrayed in statues and other artwork as being severely overweight, like a cab-driver with a pizza fetish. Seated on his cushions, he looks as if he's planted there for life, unable even to lift his bulk into a standing position. He looks happy, but he doesn't really look healthy. This is the image many people have of the Buddha. Walking by a local store awhile ago, I saw a T-shirt in the window that read, *I have the body of a god. Unfortunately it's Buddha.* This image is completely wrong. The Buddha should sue for slander.

In his youth, the Buddha was an athlete, a champion archer. As a wandering monk, he practiced asceticism for many years, starving himself to weaken his body so that his spirit could rise up from the flesh. This was a common practice in India at the time. He nearly died of starvation. He finally rejected the path of asceticism and began eating normally. He never sacrificed his health for the sake of spiritual development again. Through the rest of his life, he walked from town to town with his disciples to spread his teachings. Obesity was never a problem for the Buddha and his followers. They ate a healthy diet and got plenty of exercise.

The Buddha lived to the age of eighty, when he died of food poisoning after eating some spoiled meat. So he must have kept himself physically fit. And many of his followers lived even longer. Historically, Buddhists have been active in yoga, martial arts, and other physical activities. The Shaolin temple depicted in the TV show *Kung Fu* is an actual Chinese temple. According to legend, it was the home of Bodhidharma, the founder of Ch'an Buddhism, and he taught exercises there that would become the basis for Shaolin martial arts. A certain level of physical fitness has always been an important part of spiritual life.

Good health is an important factor in maintaining a healthy, positive attitude, because mindfulness and meditation practice depend on it. Modern ideas of holistic medicine emphasize the connections between mental, physical, and spiritual development. Everything works together. Driving the Dharma Road takes real effort in developing the body along with the mind and spirit.

Another way cabdrivers (and the rest of us) can cope with the challenges of everyday life is to develop consistent schedules that allow them to work without the danger of eventual burnout. Part of this is simply to get a good night's sleep, but of course, it doesn't stop there.

In a Zen monastery, the daily activities are strictly scheduled. It varies, but typically, everyone wakes at five, has an hour for zazen, then a half hour for breakfast, two more hours for zazen, probably with one or two periods of *kinhin,* or walking zazen, to keep the blood moving. Then an hour of work, then more zazen. There are brief periods for bathroom breaks, announced with gongs and wooden clappers. This regimentation is important because it keeps everyone focused on the activities, not thinking about what comes next and when. It also maintains order in the monastery, keeps monastic life from drifting into chaos.

Cabdriving doesn't lend itself to this kind of tight scheduling. You can't really plan it at all. Every day is different. You decide when to start and when to go home, but that's about it. Out on the streets, you go where the day takes you and you do what you can when you can.

Still, having a regular schedule is important. I sleep about the same hours every night, from about three until ten. I'm used to that: I was never a morning person. When I get up, I drink a cup of coffee, do fifteen minutes of zazen, exercise for fifteen minutes, then take a shower and get dressed. By eleven, I'm out the door and in the cab. On weekends, I stay out later at night, then sleep an extra half hour to make up for it, but the basic routine doesn't change.

Meditation, mindfulness, diet, exercise, and consistency. Call them the Five Foundations for a meaningful, healthy life behind the wheel. Or anywhere else. They all work together the way the steps on the Eightfold Path work together. But it takes determination to get started. Every New Year, people start out on diet and exercise programs that last a few days and end in a trip to the Ben and Jerry's store. In time, Zen practice can help us to develop better habits. As we build mindfulness, we can let go of the cravings and attachments that trip us up in all aspects of our daily lives. Like the *Green Acres* marathon on Nickelodeon and the Double Dish Mega-pizza with extra cheese, sausage, bacon, hamburger, and more extra cheese. These things will lose some of their appeal in time, and it will get easier to maintain healthier habits. But the time to get started on diet and nutrition is right now. It's hard at first, but life is hard. Get used to it.

. . . Hey, put down those Doritos! Get with the program.

On a Saturday evening outside a 7-Eleven on South Congress, I run in to a driver known to most of us only as 74, his cab number. He looks like Homer Simpson would look if he let himself go. He tells me he's been up for thirty-six hours, hustling fares the whole time, and he'll be out until four in the morning. The sad part is, he's proud of this. He thinks he's making a lot of money doing it this way, when all he's really doing is working a killer quadruple shift, then missing the next two days to recover. And since he's worn out most of the shift, he's not really getting much done while he's out there. Most drivers who try doing this either wise up or go away, but he's been doing this for a while and he doesn't seem to be wising up.

While he's telling me this, he's scooping nacho chips through a giant bowl of microwaved cheese food and scarfing them down with a Big Gulp of cola. That can't be good.

74 grins at me and says, "Hey, man. You want some nachos?"

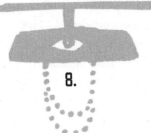

ATTENTION, ATTENTION, ATTENTION

I'm sitting in the cabstand at the Omni, waiting for something to happen, and I'm thinking about mindfulness. Zen practice can be summed up in two words: pay attention! Or: Wake up! All the meditation, the precepts, the *koans,* everything is designed to help free the mind to perceive the world as it really is. When we do that, we can see our attachments and our delusions for what they really are. And then we can perceive our true nature and rise above our suffering. Total, complete mindfulness is called enlightenment. Or so I've heard. I'm not there yet. Really, I've got a ways to go.

Out here on 8th Street, the people on the sidewalk aren't working toward any kind of enlightenment.

Everyone has a cell phone, an iPod, a newspaper, something to keep them occupied. They barely notice the world they're actually living in. A kid goes by, about thirteen, working a video game with both hands, then a woman punching buttons on some computer gadget, an organizer of some sort. People are texting and downloading, watching *Desperate Housewives* on a two-inch screen. There's a little curb where the cars come out of the Omni and cross the sidewalk, a rise only an inch high. Half the people who go past trip over this curb, then look back at it and glare. Apparently they think the curb should feel guilty for tripping them up. If there was a second curb, they'd trip over that while they were glaring at the first one.

In Zen, mindfulness is not a practical, get-through-the-day matter. Being mindful means seeing the world as it truly is, moment to moment. It means avoiding distractions and being aware of what really happens while we are living our lives. And it's also about being aware of ourselves moment to moment, and learning to understand our place in the world.

In the Buddha's time, there were no cell phones, no handheld streaming videos. Developing mindfulness was hard then. It's harder now. There's always something to do, something calling for attention. There are calls stacked up on the cell phone, schedule changes to be entered on the organizer. We're texting and downloading. The Gorgonzolla people are invading on the Xbox and someone has to lead the defense forces. There's always something. The noise level rises constantly, but no one seems to notice that it's only noise. Constant distraction is a fact of modern life.

Not all the distraction is outside. Our minds are constantly buzzing, jumping from thought to thought. Most of these thoughts have nothing to do with what's really happening in our lives at this moment. They're just noise, like static on the cab radio that keeps us from hearing what's really going on. Zen practice is designed to help us get past the inner and outer distractions to something deeper, more meaningful.

Thinking about this, I look across the street and watch as a woman comes out between the parked cars, feeling around in her purse for her keys. She steps out into the path of an oncoming Mercedes, the driver hidden behind heavily tinted glass, not paying much attention. . . .

He sees her and overreacts, swerves out a little farther into the next lane than necessary, cutting off a dented-up work truck, the driver looking out the side window at a woman in a sundress on the sidewalk. . . .

The man in the work truck sees the Mercedes just in time, swerves out a little, passes, and then looks back to give the driver the finger, mouth a few obscenities at him. . . .

He doesn't see the light ahead at the corner of Brazos going yellow, then red, and when he sees it, he hits the brake, fishtails into the intersection, and goes right through, cutting off three lanes of traffic and scattering a dozen hapless pedestrians in the far crosswalk, all of them staring at the sign ahead that says *Walk* and walking without looking around.

The truck comes to a stop in the crosswalk, and everyone involved glares at everyone else and then moves on, toward the next crisis, waiting maybe a block away.

It's like watching a *Simpsons* action sequence out here in 3-D, only the drivers have real SUVs with badly maintained brakes. And it's not nearly as funny as watching Marge chase Homer into the garage.

I'm still sitting outside the Omni, and I'm still thinking about mindfulness. In the modern world, there are so many distractions that people forget to focus on something as simple as driving a car or crossing the street. Right now, a man with a boom box walks by, sharing his musical taste with everyone in a ten-block radius. Two women in halter tops go by on the sidewalk; they look like they might be twins. There's a man wearing a sandwich board up at the corner, warning us about an imminent alien invasion. Or maybe it's another new restaurant; these days, it's hard to tell the difference. I hear a chorus of whistles, the honking of a horn behind me, someone yells, "Hey, taxi, c'mon, willya?" Oh yeah. That would be me. Guess I wasn't paying attention. How ironic.

Mindfulness isn't just a step on the way to enlightenment—it's the key to surviving this day-to-day life. Zen practice isn't meant to help us toward some kind of personal success. Zen isn't a self-help program. This isn't *Getting Rich with Zazen* or *Zen for Mortgage Bankers*. But one of the ideas behind *Dharma Road* is that mindfulness can be a great benefit in our daily lives. And if the practical benefits of Zen training can motivate us to work harder to develop a strong practice, that's all right too.

Developing mindfulness is a full-time job.

In traditional Zen practice, an art such as archery, martial arts, gardening, calligraphy, or a tea ceremony is transformed into an exercise in mindfulness. The same can be done with simple, everyday activities such as washing dishes, preparing a meal, or driving. Rituals in Zen monasteries are always performed mindfully, as are the work periods that punctuate the zazen sessions and keep things running. When a task is performed mindfully, there are no distractions, neither internal nor external. The interior voice, the stream of normal consciousness, shuts down for a while. When the calligrapher loses himself in his writing or the driver becomes one with the road, that's mindfulness.

When we concentrate fully on what we're doing, everything else falls away. Worries just vanish. Time seems to pass more quickly. You're lost in woodcarving or you're playing your guitar, and suddenly you realize that hours have passed and you feel better than you've felt in a long time. That's mindfulness.

It's like sex. When you're totally involved, the world just drops away. Nothing matters except what you're doing right at that moment. Your mind doesn't wander at all. And if it does, you're doing it wrong.

Take the activity of driving. Much of the time, any driver will function on internal autopilot: routine activities like keeping the car going in a straight line are performed almost unconsciously, while real attention is paid only when there's something important to do. Out on the highway, it doesn't take much to keep the car in its lane and maintain a normal speed, and hours can go by with the mind just wandering around, not focused on anything. City driving is more demanding, but even that requires only occasional attention.

The first step in mindful driving is to avoid distractions. Cell phones and the dispatch radio are distracting. So are passengers, but I can't really do this without them. The street scene is full of distractions. And the mind itself is a distraction. If you're daydreaming behind the wheel, you're not driving mindfully. Without distractions, the activities of driving—steering, braking, and so on—are automatic, reflexive, and don't usually need to be kept under conscious control. Even awareness of your surroundings—regular glances at the mirrors, for example—becomes automatic, a habit, simply a natural part of driving.

This is an example of the Zen concept of no-mind, the idea that the busy, distracted mind interferes in our everyday activities and does more harm than good. Even thinking about what we're doing prevents us from experiencing the world as it really is and responding to it in a natural way. The solution is to get the distractions out of the way and let the mind function naturally.

There's a great *Far Side* cartoon that illustrates the concept of no-mind. A nervous-looking man is sitting at the back of an orchestra holding a huge pair of cymbals. He's sweating bullets. He's thinking: "This time I won't screw up. I won't. I won't. . . ." The caption: "Rodney screws up."

In Eugen Herrigel's classic *Zen in the Art of Archery*, the author learns to shoot an arrow by letting go of his need to control the arrow's flight. Throughout his training, he tries to figure out what is going wrong, why he can't hit the target. His frustration grows. He's ready to give up in defeat. Then, when he stops thinking about his technique and just fires the arrow without conscious thought, he masters the art.

As the Nike ads used to say, "Just do it."

Mindfulness isn't only about focusing on the world around us. We also have to focus on ourselves. The only way to overcome distractions is to be aware of them. Usually when we're distracted, we don't even realize it. We just go from distraction to distraction without realizing what we're doing. We pull into the airport cab line and realize that we haven't really been paying attention on the way and we don't remember much of anything that happened since we left downtown. We've been daydreaming. An important part of developing mindfulness is to be more aware of what we're doing and thinking from moment to moment. It's the only way to do better. In time, we can see the daydreams coming, and we can let them go quickly and easily.

Sometimes when I'm out in the cab, just driving around, I'll focus on my own actions, feeling the pressure on the brake pedal, feeling the steering wheel turning, and then coming back. These actions are usually performed unconsciously, but focusing attention on them can be an interesting exercise. It's the same with watching the road. I occasionally practice shifting my attention between the mirrors and the road ahead, with occasional glances to the sides, although there's really nothing over there I need to see. This is a good way of developing a useful habit, leading to a better awareness of the road and the movements of the traffic.

These are really exercises to be done for occasional short periods, and only when it's safe. They can help to break the habit of distracted driving that we all fall into. But really, when I'm driving, I'm not doing any exercises at all. I'm just driving, but as in any activity, I'm trying to be aware of what I'm doing, trying to be alert, not as an exercise or even as a safety measure, but because it's the best way to do anything. It's just driving; there's nothing special about it. To paraphrase the Buddha, "When I'm driving, I know that I am driving."

Vietnamese Zen master Thich Nhat Hanh points out that in driving, the focus is usually on the destination, not on the journey. He suggests using red lights and stop signs as temple bells are used, as reminders to refocus the attention in the present and simply enjoy the ride. He says the red light is your friend, because it calls you back to the present. A good thought, but a red light is no friend to a cabdriver.

Driving in bad weather requires an extra level of mindfulness. I'm out on the road in a thunderstorm, the first rain in weeks. There's a sheen of oil coming up on the surface, sheets of rain whipping across the road, killing the visibility. Drivers are pulling to the side, lost. The passenger says, "Don't stop. My shift starts in fifteen minutes, and I really can't afford to be late again." I lean forward and focus on the road, doing twenty, totally absorbed in the street scene before me. When we pull up at our destination, I'm almost surprised to be there. That's mindfulness.

A more mundane example of mindfulness practice is the all-important trip through the self-service carwash. Washing a car is tedious, even if it's only done occasionally. Doing it every night after a twelve-hour-plus shift behind the wheel, it can become a soul-sucking bore. It's easy for the mind to wander, to just wave the foaming brush at the dirt, not really getting it going, then wander around with the wand, spraying without giving it a good rinse. I'm thinking about my shift, thinking I should have worked the radio harder, thinking . . . Then the water shuts off, and I sheepishly start feeding in more quarters, kicking myself for losing my focus. And then being distracted while I kick myself. It's also easy to move too quickly, just trying to get it over with. I'll find myself hurrying along and making mistakes, missing the mud stain on the bottom of the back door, forgetting the roof entirely. Then I have to go back over it, cursing myself for messing up and losing focus again.

The carwash is a good way of getting instant feedback. By focusing on what I'm doing, I can do the job thoroughly for eight quarters. If I'm not focused, I'll have to either feed in more quarters or take the heat for a dirty car at checkout in the morning. Of course, the money doesn't really matter. Neither does the time. Or what happens at checkout. It's all just a way of putting a little structure in my unstructured life and knowing when I'm letting my mind wander.

You don't need a cab to practice mindfulness. It doesn't have to be complicated. Another example of this practice is simply to eat a single raisin with full attention. First, examine the raisin carefully. Take your time. Study its color, its texture, the patterns on its surface. Move it around in the fingers to feel its skin. Squeeze it gently. Sniff it: it's not really odorless. Then place it on your tongue and move it around in your mouth, feeling it warming up and softening. Bite into it once and feel the sweet juice ooze out onto your tongue. Bite a few more times, then chew, feeling the way it breaks up and the taste spreads through your mouth. Finally, swallow it. Eaten this way, a raisin becomes a miracle of sensation, a revelation.[1]

---

1 This exercise is adapted from *The Mindful Way through Depression* by Mark Williams, John Teasdale, Zindel Segal, and Jon Kabat-Zinn (New York: The Guilford Press, 2007).

When we shovel a handful of raisins in and chomp down on them, we miss all that. And most of our experiences are shoveled in while our minds are on something else entirely.

Every moment brings an opportunity to practice mindfulness. Eating a raisin. Washing the dishes. Checking the fluid levels, changing a flat. Whatever comes up. Our lives are filled with simple, everyday activities. They can be practiced as an exercise in mindfulness, or they can be done mindlessly. It's up to you.

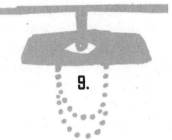

SITTING, NOT THINKING

In the morning, I get up around nine thirty, maybe ten, depending on when I got home the night before. I have some coffee, take a shower, water the plants. It's like anyone's morning. A little later than some, but it doesn't feel that way to me. Then I spend fifteen or twenty minutes on a cushion, clearing my mind. Meditating. Preparing for the day.

Later in the day, I'll get out of the cab and sit on a bench for a few minutes. I'll just let everything go for a while and then get back to work.

Sometimes, sitting at a light in the cab, I'll just take a few deep breaths and let them out slowly. I'll feel the tension going out with the breaths. It's all meditation.

Meditation isn't something you'd usually associate with cabdriving. It's hard to imagine Travis Bickle doing deep *samadhi* on the cot in his rented room. It's like Keith Richards leading a Bible study group. It could happen, but it's not something you'd expect to see. Although it might have done Travis some good. Keith too, for that matter.

Meditation is the most important tool in the kit for developing mindfulness. It helps free the mind from its usual state of distraction and open it up to the richness of our everyday lives. It's like a cleansing rest for the mind. A reset button for the soul. It's the heart of Zen practice.

The word *Zen* is Japanese for "meditation." By its very nature, Zen practice is a meditation practice. All schools of Buddhism teach the importance of following the precepts, learning the sutras, developing compassion for others, and developing mindfulness through meditation, but in Zen the emphasis is placed directly on meditation. It's the central feature of any Zen practice, from hardscrabble cabdriver Zen like mine to the most disciplined monastic Zen.

When Siddhartha sat down under a simple fig tree and vowed to remain until he became enlightened, it was intensive meditation that allowed him to break the chains of conditioning and perceive the world as it truly is. Despite the importance of meditation in his own development, the Buddha was not primarily a meditation teacher. Meditation practice was so common in his world that it may never have occurred to him that people would need more than the most basic instruction. Today a broad range of schools (in almost every spiritual and religious tradition) teach a wide variety of meditation practices.

The Buddha's enlightenment is the defining event in the history of Buddhism. Zen tries to recreate this event for everyone by using a refined version of the approach the Buddha used. The form of meditation used in Zen is called *zazen,* which is Japanese for "sitting meditation."

It's as simple as breathing and one of the most difficult activities there is. Zazen is a way of quieting the mind while maintaining full awareness. There are many practical benefits to the practice of zazen. It helps the mind to develop a focus on everyday activities. It can help promote calmness, peace of mind, a wider perspective on everyday life, and a higher level of personal effectiveness. It's also the proven way to attain enlightenment.

But zazen is not practiced with any goal in mind. This is not a self-help program, a way of becoming a better cabdriver or a better person. Or even a buddha. The practice of zazen should be rewarding in itself. It should be enough. Shunryu Suzuki said that zazen is itself enlightenment, that there is nothing more to be gained beyond this simple practice.

These simple instructions should be enough to help anyone to get started on a basic Zen practice, although it's best to seek out personal instruction if it's available.

Zazen should be practiced in a quiet room, with soft, steady lighting. Don't use candles: they flicker. Wear loose, comfortable clothing. Try to avoid distractions. Choose a time when you won't be disturbed. Put out the dog and take the phone off the hook.

The first step in zazen is to take a comfortable and stable posture. There is a great emphasis on posture in Zen practice. Poor posture leads to distractions. The body sags, sways; the muscles get sore, sloppiness sets in. So good zazen starts with good posture. If the body is stable, the mind will follow.

The full lotus position is preferred over all others. Sit cross-legged on a cushion (called a *zafu*), with the right foot placed on the left thigh, the left foot on the right thigh. The back is held straight, the head lifted up, the chin pulled in. This posture is very stable, very balanced, and it may be held for long periods of time.

I can't do a full lotus. I can't come close. I don't think I know anyone who can. Trying to fold myself up into any lotus at all leads to hilarious and sometimes painful results. My legs just don't fold that way. I sit in the *seiza* position, a kneeling posture with the knees a little spread, butt resting on the zafu. A small bench can be used in place of the zafu. This posture is not ideal, but it is very comfortable, very stable, and won't cause serious bodily injury. And if you like, you can take up yoga to loosen up those legs.

Some people cannot sit in the seiza posture either. People with back problems or other health issues can't maintain this posture and are encouraged to use a chair, sitting as straight as possible. People with severe physical problems have performed long periods of zazen while lying flat on their backs, although this is really only a last resort. Although posture is important, zazen in any posture is better than no zazen at all. Remember: it's not your body that sits in zazen, it's your mind.

One posture that should always be avoided is the conventional cross-legged posture, with the shins crossed, the feet resting on the floor. This posture is unstable, distracting and, in the long run, uncomfortable.

In any posture, the shoulders are held up firmly with the arms hanging loosely to the sides. The hands are held together over the navel in a position known as the cosmic *mudra*. To form the mudra, hold the hands together with the palms up, the fingers of the left hand resting on the fingers of the right. The thumbs are held up, the tips touching, to form an oval. The mudra should be formed with care, but once it is formed, the hands should be held in a relaxed manner.

The Soto Zen style is to sit facing a blank wall. (My practice is more or less Soto Zen.) In the Rinzai school, they sit in the same posture, but facing out into the room. In either case, the eyes should be kept half closed—and half open—and looking slightly downward.

Don't worry too much about the details. A good way to get started is just to sit in a kitchen chair with your hands folded. It's simple and straightforward. Posture and setting are important, but the most important thing is to get started—then make an effort to do better. The rest will take care of itself. I have done zazen on a pile of newspapers and on a sleeping bag in a stuff sack. I do short zazen sessions sitting in the front seat of the cab in the airport line. Use what you have. Do your best with it. Make it work for you. Remember, right effort is one of the steps on the Eightfold Path. Right equipment is not.

Once the posture is taken, the attention is focused on the breath. Breathing normally, count the exhalations, one, two, three . . . up to ten, then begin again. When thoughts arise, just let them go without attaching to them. As simple as this sounds, it's actually hard to do. Thoughts appear constantly, and it's not easy to let them go. The count is lost, then started again. Now there's an itch, the sound of a car going by. The count is lost, start again. Now there's a pain in one knee, a slouch creeping into the posture. Straighten up. How long has it been? Start again. This can go on for some time and the beginner might not get past a count of three or four. This is a lesson in itself. The mind has a will of its own. It's not entirely *your* mind. It takes patience and perseverance to quiet it down.

Meditation is like fishing. There's a fine line between doing zazen and just sitting around doing nothing. It's important to stay focused, alert. Don't become distracted, and most of all, don't doze off. It all gets easier with practice, but daydreaming and napping are not practice. They're just daydreaming and napping.

There are some tricks that help the mind to focus. After settling myself on the cushion, I generally start by taking a deep breath, holding it a beat, then exhaling very slowly through pursed lips. Like whistling, without the sound. I repeat this twice more, then resume normal breathing. This is called a straw breath. It provides a definite starting point for the session and helps get the attention focused quickly. During zazen, when my mind begins to wander, I'll take a deep breath, then let it out slowly through pursed lips in small sips. I do this twice more, then resume. This is the bamboo breath. It forces the mind to refocus actively on the breath.

It's natural to inhale, exhale, then pause and begin again. Pausing after the inhalation forces the mind to refocus on the breath. Tricks like this can help to keep the focus for a longer time, but they are only tricks. The real practice is to remain focused for long periods without resorting to tricks.

Counting is also just a trick. After a while, the numbers get in the way and zazen becomes easier without counting at all. A good way to get past the numbers is to use smaller and smaller counts. Eventually, the count can be reduced to one. Then the count will drop away completely. This is called *shikantaza*, "just sitting." Thoughts arise, then fade, and we just sit and watch them, let them go. Doing this, we start to understand ourselves a little better. We feel the thoughts floating around inside us. We get a sense of what our minds are doing.

It's customary to bow three times at the end of a session. This bow is a gesture to Buddha and to the world, a way of letting go of the ego. Bow deeply from the waist, with the hands kept together in the mudra. Bow like you mean it, with your whole mind and body. This is also a more graceful way to close the session than just getting up and leaving.

It's best to set aside a regular time of day for zazen, a time when you won't be interrupted. I sit for fifteen minutes or so in the morning, then ten or fifteen more before bed. Sometimes I do zazen for a few minutes in the cab, or sitting on a bench by the sidewalk when there's not much else to do. Once a week, usually on Saturday afternoon, I set aside some extra time for zazen, a half hour or more. The schedule you set doesn't matter as much as the fact that there is a schedule, that there is a regular, constant practice and a commitment to keep the practice going.

With some practice, it's possible to attain a state of deep concentration called *samadhi*, in which the mind is quiet, undisturbed, but attentive at the same time. The real point of practice is to maintain something like an active samadhi in everyday life. The result is a mindful awareness of the unfolding of our lives and a sense of involvement in the mundane, everyday activities that we usually pay little attention to.

In *The Compass of Zen*, Seung Sahn illustrates the dedication involved in Zen practice by describing a cat on the trail of a mouse. The cat chases the mouse into a hole and then waits for it to come out. While it waits, there is no thought in the cat's mind except the thought of the mouse in the hole, no distraction from its purpose. Its eyes are wide open, its tail twitches, its fur stands up. It sits like a coiled spring, ready to strike. An hour goes by, two hours. When the mouse appears, the cat will be ready. Zazen is like this, except there is no mouse. That focus is widened to include the whole world.

The key to building a strong Zen practice is to make a consistent effort to fit meditation and mindfulness into everyday life. My practice is the best I can manage with the work schedule I have and my other limitations. In some ways, it would be better to give up the life I have and check into a monastery or move into a secluded Himalayan cave. But that's not going to happen. In today's world, most people have to develop a practice that fits with their other activities. That's all right. The key is to make the effort, to do what you can while you can, and then build from there.

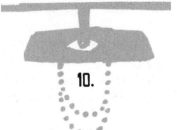

STOP AND SMELL THE HOT JAVA

Buddhism is full of psychology. It's like a dose of Dr. Phil for the soul. A disturbing number of books about Buddhism are written by psychotherapists. It makes you wonder. Regardless, working to keep a positive attitude is only the beginning of a successful practice. We've spent years developing complex personalities, full of conflicts and delusions that get in the way of our true nature. We have to do a certain amount of work on ourselves to make real growth possible. And we want to do it without spending years in therapy. Because we're too busy for that.

An important part of practice is the development of personal qualities that make spiritual progress possible. Personal growth is the heart of Buddhist practice. The personal qualities that promote spiritual growth are known as the *paramitas,* or "perfections."

The original Six Paramitas are:

1. Generosity: Avoiding attachments and living our lives for the benefit of others.

2. Conduct: Living the precepts that define morality and ethics, not just following the rules.

3. Patience: Taking things as they come and making progress, however slowly.

4. Effort: Putting practice first and maintaining it against all obstacles.

5. Meditation: Working to deepen and strengthen the meditation practice.

6. Wisdom: Always learning from experience and growing in understanding.

The paramitas are related to the precepts and the steps on the Eightfold Path. Everything works together. On the path, right action is defined by adherence to the precepts. And effort, meditation, and wisdom relate directly to steps on the path. The steps on the path are about behavior: they spell out actions to be taken. The paramitas are about character. They are about who we want to be.

Taken together, the paramitas describe the character of the bodhisattva, whose goal is to use spiritual practice to save all beings from their suffering. This level of self-lessness is the ideal of all forms of Mahayana practice, which include Tibetan and Ch'an Buddhism as well as Zen. The Bodhisattva Vows are recited at temples and centers all over the world. Part of the bodhisattva ideal is a pledge to forgo complete enlightenment until all beings are saved. The bodhisattva will not attempt to escape the wheel of life and death, but will return again and again to this life of suffering to help others. In its broadest definition, a bodhisattva is anyone who has set foot on the path to enlightenment. Even without the vows. Just by reading *Dharma Road* you have become a bodhisattva. Congratulations. Now you can begin to save all beings.

Some traditions have ten paramitas, an example of a list being changed to fit the decimal system. The lists don't always agree with each other. Some of the qualities that have been added to the original six include renunciation, truthfulness, equanimity, aspiration, unselfish love (*metta*) and knowledge. They're all fine qualities, but six are probably enough for us to work on.

I'm working on the paramita of patience. Developing patience is a challenge for me. A big one. I am not by nature a patient man. I never have been. I hate to be kept on hold or told to wait in line. I will not take a number. I do not enjoy the music while my party is being reached. I can't stand paper-shuffling, take-a-meeting people. I'm temperamentally unqualified for government work and pretty much anything else that doesn't come with a gas pedal of some kind to speed things up. Instant gratification takes too long for me. When it comes to spiritual practice, I want to be enlightened today and I want all those other beings to get with the program so we can all escape the wheel of life and death by the end of the week. I know I have to calm down to make progress, that I have to develop qualities of patience and perseverance in myself. I'm trying, but it doesn't come easily.

Impatience can be a virtue for a cabdriver. You have to keep things moving out there to make a living. But it can lead to trouble. It can lead to ulcers, high blood pressure, temper tantrums, and wrecked cabs. I know this, and I'm doing what I can. I make a real effort to keep myself under control when I'm driving, but the truth is I just want to get moving, no matter where I am or what I'm doing.

I'm in Whole Foods, standing at the coffee counter at the start of my day, treating myself to an extra large Colombian for the road. I just need a little cream and sugar. It should just take a second, but there's a woman in front of me, studying the array of sweeteners. She adds a dash of soy milk, carefully pours a little unrefined sugar out from the shaker, stirs it twenty times, and takes a careful sip. Not satisfied, she adds a much smaller dab of soy milk, stirs it twenty times, and takes another sip. Now she picks up the sugar shaker, very, very carefully pours just a few grains into the coffee, stirs it twenty times, and takes another sip.

This is why I leave the pepper spray behind when I get out of the cab. It's why I don't think concealed handguns should be legal. (In Texas, they are.) I take a deep breath, try to think happy thoughts.

As she picks up the sugar shaker yet again, I take a deep, cleansing breath, hold it for a moment, then exhale slowly in small sips, bamboo-style. The Zen version of counting to ten. I focus on the feel of the air flowing over my tongue and through my lips, letting go, calming down.

A little digression here: wouldn't this woman be better off changing her own attitude, opening herself to the taste of the coffee as it is and enjoying that instead of trying to adjust the taste so it's exactly the way she likes it? At least it would still be hot.

Now she's discovered the shaker of cinnamon. She's studying it, now pouring a little out, very experimentally, now stirring another twenty times. Now I'm taking another bamboo breath, feeling myself relaxing, opening to the bakery smells, the sounds of the people moving past me, the Beach Boys singing "God Only Knows" on the store's sound system. I lose myself for a moment in the harmony. If I hadn't taken a moment, I might have missed that. Now she's sipping again, trying to get it just so, and my coffee's getting cold in my hand, the paper cup not providing enough insulation, and I'm getting upset about that and taking another bamboo breath, just trying to get through this.

Finally, she's satisfied and moves away, giving me a little smile and mumbling an apology she doesn't really feel. I cream and sugar my own coffee, cap it, and get in the express line at the checkout. Ahead of me there's a discussion about a vegetable no one can identify, then someone is writing a check, there's an ID inspection, someone else is way over the ten-item limit. I'm taking so many bamboo breaths by now, I'm hyperventilating. By the time I'm out of the store, I've got lukewarm coffee and the start of a headache. It's eleven o'clock in the morning, and I'll be out on the streets for the next fifteen hours.

Patience is not high on the list of qualities you'd expect to find in a cabdriver. For me, it's a hard one to master anyway, and the truth is, driving a cab doesn't help. I'm thinking about the fares I'm missing while I'm standing in line, and it drives me nuts. Of course, there's a simple solution. If I never got out of the cab, I'd never miss a fare. I can almost see myself trying that. But then I'd never develop the paramita of patience.

It takes some perspective to get through the day. I have to accept that there are trade-offs in life. If I'm going to get a coffee to go at Whole Foods, it's going to take a little time. I could try the Stop 'n' Rob, but they make a dozen pots at six in the morning, then leave them out all day. Before long, they're undrinkable. But there's no line at the coffee counter.

Out on the road, it just gets harder. I'm riding down the interstate when traffic bogs down and I'm sitting helplessly in a sea of cars. Then the dispatcher starts handing out calls, and I can't take one because I have no idea when I'll be able to pick it up. When the traffic clears, the dispatcher is taking a smoke break, so I won't be getting a fare for a while. This is why so many cabdrivers throw their keys in a storm drain and walk away.

Looking around in traffic, I can see the other drivers stewing in their own cars, glaring at each other as they sit there texting, reading the paper, waiting to move. They're all late for something, and they don't like it. It's hard on everybody.

Life is full of trade-offs. Spend time in line to get a decent cup of coffee or do without. Get on the interstate and hope the traffic keeps moving or take the streets and drive slower. You take your chances. There's nothing we can do to change it. All we can do is get used to it.

The paramitas really refer to the development of personal qualities as a step toward spiritual growth, not as a way to make city life bearable. Of course, there's no real difference between everyday life and Zen practice. So being patient behind the wheel and in other day-to-day situations is as much a part of practice as reading the sutras or sitting zazen. I'm not going to race through to buddhahood in one sudden burst of acceleration, as much as I'd like that. It's going to take time, and I'll have to accept that and keep trying. Because I don't plan to give up.

I might as well slow down and enjoy the journey.

The frustrations of everyday life are hard to avoid without checking into a monastery or a psych ward, and most of us aren't going to sign up for either. But we can try to avoid the emotional attachments that cause so many problems for us. In order to practice Zen, we have to let go of some of the drama in our lives. Practice gives us a chance to see beyond our attachments and take things as they are. I remember reading a book on Zen practice that referred to day-to-day events as the scenery of our lives. It's interactive, but it's still scenery. We should try to find a way to appreciate the scenery without letting it drive us nuts. Finding it just takes practice. And, ironically, patience.

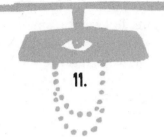

GET A GRIP

Cabdriving is like an episode of *The Simpsons*. You're watching Homer wrapping Ned Flanders's house in toilet paper to get even for something, and you go to the kitchen to get a beer. Or a nice cup of herbal tea. When you come back, Homer is in a space bubble orbiting the moon. And you wonder, *What happened? How did he get there?*

Sometimes it's like a case of bipolar disorder. You're cruising, raking in the fares one moment, then it all goes bad for a while. It's up and down, all day long. Most of the passengers are nice—regular people—some of them are toxic jerks. Sometimes the traffic just flows along, and sometimes it clogs up and dies. When things are going well, you know it can't last. When it comes apart, you know that can't last either. It's a life of constant change. All you can do is try to keep yourself on an even keel while it goes by.

It's pretty much like everything else in this life.

It's a Friday morning, around ten. I'm out a little early today, working downtown, thinking I'm going to push it a little, make a real day of it. I've been slacking off lately, but no more. Today I'm a samurai cabdriver, a real road warrior. I will not be denied. I pull up at the Four Seasons, load three women going out to Highland Mall for some shopping, then load two men at the Red Lion, take them up to Dell headquarters, then take a call out at Seton Northwest Hospital, take a patient home on a voucher, headed farther north. Now I'm about twenty miles from downtown, and five minutes later, I get a call at Lakeline Mall. Two men with suitcases get in and say, "We're going to the Hyatt."

That's downtown.

This is how cabdriving is supposed to be. Straight-forward. Drop someone off, pick someone else up. Every trip gets the meter turning over. None of these just-down-the-block rides. No sitting outside a 7-Eleven, waiting for something to happen. I know it's not going to last. It never does.

I pull up at a red light on Research Boulevard, look around. On an empty lot a half block away, there's a bill-board for a pharmaceutical testing company soliciting test subjects. It reads: *Have you been diagnosed with schizophrenia?* Sitting at the light, I look up at the sign and think: *Not yet.*

When I drop the men off at the Hyatt, there are four cabs lined up in the lot, waiting. I figure I'll ride around, check the cabstands. I wave to the drivers, head for the exit. Then it all goes bad. As soon as I pull out of the Hyatt, an Austin Police cruiser appears in the rearview mirror. His light bars come on, strobing like mad. I'm doing about five, so I know I'm not speeding. I haven't cut anyone off. I've only gone fifty feet down Barton

Springs Road, and he can't be pulling me over for something I did in the Hyatt parking lot. At least I don't think he can. I'm not really sure. I think, irrationally, maybe he just wants to get by. Oh, yeah, that happens all the time. I pull off into a parking lot, and he comes in behind me.

He walks up, looks at my driver's license, my hack license, and the cab's registration, playing it up a little, looking like he's suspicious. He studies the insurance form taped to the windshield. He's a young guy, with the real dark, shiny shades, the police posture. He hands the papers back.

"Sir," he says in the police voice, polite but not planning on a discussion, "were you aware that you were not wearing your seat belt?"

My seat belt? I think fast. As fast as I can under the circumstances. I'm a little rattled. Was I? What? Suddenly I don't feel that smart. "Well, I'd just dropped a couple guys off back there and I, uh, hadn't put it back on. I was going to."

"So you had to get out of the car, that was why your belt was off?"

I'm still trying to think fast. He might have seen me at the Hyatt, so he'll know if I lie about it. Or maybe not. In these situations, lying is almost automatic; everyone lies to traffic cops. He knows that. He's been listening to lame excuses all morning. Mine aren't going to be any better than anyone else's. Of course, now there's another problem. I've spent so much time thinking about a simple yes-or-no question that anything I say will sound like a lie. Besides, aren't Buddhists supposed to tell the truth? Isn't that what right speech is all about?

"No, I didn't get out of the car. I just turned around and talked to them for a few seconds, had the seat belt off. I guess it just slipped my mind after that." Which is close enough to the truth. Really, I haven't used a seat belt since driver's ed.

"Sir, did you know that you are 50 percent more likely to survive an accident when you're wearing a seat belt?"

"I know that, yeah. Well, not the 50 percent part, but I know I should wear the belt. I'll try to do better." I give him a hopeful look, but he already has his ticket book open, pen going. "Does this go on my driving record?" I ask weakly. I don't think I can stand another session of comedy defensive driving school to clear another ticket. It just isn't that funny the third or fourth time around.

"No, sir, this is not a moving violation, and it won't go on your record." He shows me the ticket, points out the address of the Municipal Court, which is really not necessary, me being a cabdriver and all, tells me I have three weeks to pay it.

Then I ask him the other big question. "How much is this going to cost me?"

"I don't know how much these tickets are. I just write them. Personally, I'd rather be out catching criminals, but this is my assignment for the day, so I'm doing it. Remember, seat belts save lives." He smiles down at me, turns away, then looks over his shoulder. "Have a nice day," he adds. Maybe he's being sarcastic: I can't tell.

Sitting in the lot, staring at the ticket, I feel like I've been body slammed by the Incredible Hulk. My mind is racing. This is the remains of the samurai cabdriver—gutted and sliced, left lying in the sun for the vultures to feed on. I have been denied. I am now the man without the plan, the rebel without a clue. This cop is spending his day writing up seat belt tickets, and he doesn't know how much the tickets cost? Give me a break. If it were any reasonable amount, he'd just tell me. This is going to be bad. My big weekend is already wiped out. I'll have to hustle until Monday just to cover the ticket. Taking on the world, my ass. It's not even noon, and the world already has my ass in a jar.

I'm crushed. It takes me five minutes just to get out of the lot and back on the road. Finally, I head for the Four Seasons and park in the stand behind four other cabs, things suddenly looking bleak all around. A horse-drawn carriage pulls up next to me. The horse stops and takes a dump on the pavement. Then he twists his head around and laughs at me.

Okay, maybe he's not laughing. Maybe it's more like a whinny. From where I'm sitting, he's laughing at me and I don't like it. I'd wring his neck, but he's pretty big. He starts walking again. I get out of the cab and sit on a stone bench, thinking about the money I've just wasted, wondering what the hell I'm doing out here, thinking I might as well go out and sit at the airport, wait for something to happen out there. Or take up a less stressful line of work. Cabdrivers have been known to just walk away from their cabs, leave the keys in and the motor running and go home, never come back. I know the feeling.

I know, you're thinking, *This guy's a Zen Buddhist? He's meditating, developing a wider view of the world, getting it all in perspective?* You're thinking I'm a half step from a ride in the nut wagon. That's cabdriving. If you want to calm down and learn to live a more peaceful life, try cabdriving. If you can keep your mind out here, you'll be fine.

If I was living any normal life, I'd be the serene messenger of peace from the planet of bliss. The calm center of the storm. Mr. Composure. But I'm not living a normal life. I'm a cabdriver. I'm a little on edge most of the time.

I take a few cleansing breaths. Deep ones. I ask myself, what would the Buddha do? Well, he probably wouldn't let himself get stuck in such a dead-end piss pot way to make a living. I feel like a pile of stepped-on crap. I keep trying. What would the Buddha do?

He'd probably know enough to wear his seat belt. That's what he'd do.

After a while, I think of a cliché: when life gives you lemons, make lemon meringue pie. Well, something like that. Every cloud has a silver lining. I'm disgusted. I wasn't always like this. All this mindfulness and meditation practice, and I'm coming up with ideas that belong on tacky wall posters.

Then I have a thought. I feel a little shift in my point of view. I can suddenly taste some of that meringue, see a little silver in the overcast. There's something in this that might help. If I let it. Here I am driving two hundred miles a day in city traffic, going out on the interstate with the big rigs, surrounded by some of the worst excuses for amateur drivers on the planet. Most of the time, I'm stressed out, in a hurry. And the fact is, I've never used my seat belt. Even pulling out of the lot after staring at the seat belt ticket for five minutes, I hadn't strapped in. I've never been in an accident in my entire life, but if I'm going to drive a cab, the odds are stacked high against me. And like the man said, seat belts do save lives. Maybe I could save mine.

Now I'm feeling better. I'm out a hundred dollars or more (it turned out to be a hundred and fifty), but I have a new plan. From now on, I'll wear the seat belt at all times and someday, for that money, I'll save my own life.

AC-AC-AC-AC . . .

There's a great scene in the classic sitcom *Taxi*. Louie, the dispatcher, played by Danny DeVito, is showing a rookie driver around the garage, telling him how things are done. Some of the drivers—probably Alex, Tony, and Elaine, maybe Bobby—are sitting around playing cards, waiting for something to happen. The drivers all spent a lot of time sitting around at the garage on that show. They played a lot of cards. That isn't really how the cab industry works. I guess if they just came in, got in their cabs and left, it wouldn't have been much of a show.

Louie tells the rookie, "There's one word I never, ever want to hear in this garage." He looks over at the drivers. "Hey, losers," he says, "what is the one word I never want to hear in my garage?"

The drivers just shrug, roll their eyes. They don't know what he's talking about. They don't care.

"See," Louie says to the rookie. "See that? They all know better than to say that word in my garage."

The word is *accident*.

Or, as Louie says it, "Ac-ac-ac-ac . . ." Even he can't say the word in the garage.

Short of being shot, an accident is the worst thing that can happen to a cabdriver. Even a minor fender bender can be a life-changing experience. First of all, you're on the hook for a repair bill. And it's never cheap. While cabs are well-insured, the policies generally include a thousand-dollar deductible. And the repairs always seem to come out very close to the deductible. So you're out a thousand dollars. Which, in the cab industry, is real money. Plus, you're unemployed, at least until the cab is fixed or you can line up another one.

On an average day in the United States, 122 people die in traffic accidents. It's like a plane going down every day. Some days, it's a small commuter plane. Other days—the Fourth of July, New Years Eve, for example—it's a well-loaded 747. Traffic accidents are the leading cause of death for Americans aged four to thirty-four. And those are just the fatalities. Many more are injured, some seriously, some for life.

There are two main causes for auto accidents: driver error and pure chance.

Studies have shown that driver errors caused by inattention are at least partially to blame for as many as 80 percent of all auto accidents. That includes drunk driving and drowsiness. Cell phone use while driving has been shown to be just as dangerous as driving drunk. (Watch out for drunks with cell phones—they're lethal.) And that's only part of the problem. People are eating, talking, fixing their hair and makeup, shaving (with an electric razor, I hope), changing stations on the radio, fooling with the text-messaging camera phone, watching the world go by out the side window. And much of the time, they're daydreaming, not thinking about what they're doing at all. Given that so much of driving is second nature, it's an easy habit to fall into. And it's dangerous.

Better driving can be a side benefit of Zen practice. By cutting down on the distractions and driving with mindfulness and focus, we'll just be more effective out on the road. And safer. If safer driving can add a little motivation to develop a consistent Zen practice, so much the better. Whatever works. But even if you're not working toward any kind of self-realization, it's a good idea to stay focused out on the road. Skip that last beer. Leave the cell phone off for a while. If you're sleepy, just go home. In fact, take a cab.

But no matter how mindful the driver, there's still pure chance. Sometimes a tire blows on an overpass or a mule deer runs out in the highway and freezes. Or a drunk driver in a semi loses control coming the other way on a two-lane highway. Doing ninety. Sometimes there's nothing a driver can do but close his eyes and wish he was home in bed. No one is really safe.

It's a dangerous world. It's not just the traffic. Bad things happen to good people. Life is filled with potholes. We can go in for a routine physical and spend the rest of our life suffering from a grim and incurable disease. We can walk out the front door of a zendo and be killed by a piece from a falling satellite. Or we can just be pushed and pulled by the random events of our everyday life, dragged down one day, lifted up the next. There's nothing we can do about that. It's random. It's the life we have, and we have to make what we can of it. We can't control the world around us to make it completely safe.

But we can take reasonable precautions. And we can do something about ourselves, about the way we deal with the randomness of everyday life. When things go wrong, the way we deal with that defines who we really are. What we're made of.

Zen teacher Ezra Bayda and his wife were stricken with autoimmune diseases caused by DDT pollution that leached into the organic garden they'd spent years developing. It was a frightening ordeal for both of them. Many people would have given in to despair at the cruel irony of it. But they were able to recover after a long struggle and use the ordeal as a learning experience. A central feature of Bayda's teaching has been to help others to deal with the struggles of their own lives.

Life is a series of accidents. There are good ones—including the fact that we are alive at all—and there are life-crushing disasters. It's important to do what we can to stay safe. We don't have to tempt fate. We can drive safely and mindfully, avoiding the distractions that create so much havoc on the roads. We can maintain a healthy lifestyle. We can manage our day-to-day lives as carefully as possible. But when it all goes wrong, we have to deal with that as well. The way we respond to the accidents that fill our lives is more important than the accidents themselves. And more within our control.

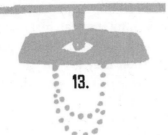

CROSSTOWN TRAFFIC

If you want to develop mindfulness, there are several options. First, you can join a monastery. This is the traditional way. For thousands of years, seekers have left their lives behind to take up a new life of contemplation and meditation. Little by little, they peel away the layers of delusion that have kept them from seeing the world as it truly is. This way has been proven again and again.

Another way is to spend twelve to sixteen hours a day out on the city streets, flowing through the traffic, seeing the way things move. Practicing mindfulness. This way has not been proven by thousands of years of experience. It's just an adventure.

Not all spiritual practice is about peaceful contemplation. The martial arts are based largely on mindfulness practices. The goal is really to keep your head under extreme conditions and react to the action without becoming distracted. That's cabdriving. Staying focused on the city streets and getting from place to place without getting stuck. It's like a Jackie Chan movie set out in the traffic.

The rookies think they're pretty good drivers. Kings of the road. They think they can just mash the gas pedal into the floorboard and keep it there until they either arrive or crash. Then they get bogged down in traffic, beaten by the mazes of one-way streets and four-way intersections, and before long, they realize there's more to it than knowing how to steer and work the gas pedal. The real cabdrivers learn to get it done on real streets, in real traffic. They plan ahead, react to road conditions as they come up, watch out for potential delays.

It's all about focus. Mindfulness. If you're sitting at a green light fiddling with the buttons on the radio, you're spinning your wheels. If you forget to change lanes until you reach the street you want to turn into, you're just a road hazard for everyone else. Next time, take a bus. Or call a cab.

You hear stories about the wild drivers, the ones who push it all the time. I picked one up at the airport. He told me he'd been a cabdriver for eight months and had piled up fourteen traffic tickets. Then they fired him. He told me he'd gotten one of the tickets for driving on the sidewalk. He also told me—just being helpful—that I was driving too slowly, that I'd never make any money that way.

When I first started driving, a driver told me with a wicked grin, "If you go fast enough, they can't get the number off the cab to report you." He was a great guy to hang around with, a lot of fun. He didn't last that long either.

City driving is really a matter of strategy, and the cabdrivers pick up some good ideas about how to move around without risking tickets and accidents.

Planning is one of the keys to city driving. Before you start out, think about the route you plan to take, taking into account the bottlenecks and other delays you're likely to run into. Know the traffic and how it changes with the time of day. At rush hour, some of the main arteries are nothing but parking lots, while there are residential streets a few blocks away with no traffic on them at all. Be flexible. If the route you're taking isn't working out, look for alternatives. If you can see a problem six blocks ahead, don't wait until you get there to look for another route. And remember to use back alleys and parking lots if they'll get you out of a traffic jam. But don't ever use sidewalks.

Watch for buses, UPS trucks, anything likely to block the road. Avoid bicycles. Watch the lights on the cross streets ahead so you'll know when they're about to change. Get off the line quickly when the light changes. When making a right turn at a red light, remember: It's just a stop sign. Don't sit there.

Sounds simple, doesn't it?

Of course it's simple. This is cabdriving, not Chinese quantum mechanics.

I know. You're disappointed. It's all common sense. You thought there was some cabdriver magic that you could use to get across town in minutes at rush hour. You thought there was some big secret the cabdrivers all knew and no one else could figure out. But it's simple: plan your route, and don't get stuck behind UPS trucks. You knew that.

But that's the point. There's no magic, no secret knowledge. What there is, is mindfulness. Of course you know enough not to get stuck behind a UPS truck. But do you notice the truck from three blocks away? Do you think to change lanes then? Or do you wait until you're stuck, and then curse the driver as he gets out with an armful of packages and a big grin? You can't think that far ahead if you're talking on the cell phone or thinking about what you should have said to your boyfriend when he gave you a couple of tickets to a monster truck rally for your birthday. You can't think that far ahead unless you're paying attention.

It's all about focus. Mindfulness. You can think of cabdriving as an epic martial arts adventure. You're up against the evil amateur drivers. They try to slow you down, block you in, force you from your route. But you don't let them. You see their moves coming from three blocks away, and you anticipate. You're too fast for them. You flow through the traffic. Unstoppable.

And it's all mindfulness.

You really can't reduce city driving to a simple set of rules to follow out on the road. Nothing in life is that simple. The key to city driving is keeping your mind open and alert, being aware of everything going on around you. For a cabdriver, practicing mindfulness on the streets is simply the best way to do the job. You have to be productive out there or you won't make any money. But it's also a way of using work as an opportunity for personal growth. In time, the focus becomes automatic. You get behind the wheel, pull out onto the streets, and it's there. And when you're not driving, it's still there. Focus.

It's not really a choice between monastic life and cabdriving. Any activity will do. Whatever you do, you can find ways to use it to develop a stronger focus, a habit of mindfulness. Your work will benefit—and in the end, so will you.

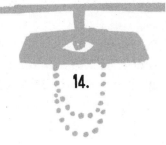

WHAT I LIKE

A central feature of Zen Buddhism is the idea that the solid, unchanging self we experience is an illusion. We focus on ourselves as separate individuals, distinct from each other and from the world around us. But when examined closely, the individual self is revealed to be no more than a collection of delusions. An illusion.

The great teacher Dogen Zenji, who studied Zen in China and established it in Japan, described this aspect of Zen in one of the best-known passages of the Zen canon: "To study the Way is to study the self. To study the self is to forget the self. To forget the self is to be enlightened by all things of the universe." In other words, to study the self is to reveal that our usual idea of it is only an illusion. Once we see this, it is an easy matter to let go of our attachments and live in true freedom.

Our likes and dislikes are a great example of this. Our personalities consist in part of long lists of things we like, things we don't like, and things we don't care about. We're attached to them, and we think they define us. They don't.

I love to listen to music. I grew up on rock and roll. Now I listen mostly to jazz. Sometimes when I'm coming back from a long trip out of town, I'll find a jazz show on the radio and just smile all the way back. I like everything from solo piano to big band and most of what's in between. I'm a huge Coltrane fan. That avant-garde jazz everyone hates? I love it. I'll listen to blues, reggae, folk, country, even zydeco. I love them all. I don't like hip-hop, opera, and whatever that stuff is that passes for pop these days. I like classical well enough, but I've never really gotten interested in it.

All these things are not good and not bad. Good and bad are only labels we attach to our experiences. They're something extra. Some things we enjoy, some we don't. That's all. What we enjoy says a lot about our lives, our experiences. It doesn't say much about music, art, literature, or anything else. I like chocolate milk. I like coffee. I don't like soft drinks—except ginger ale and root beer. I like those.

I don't like seafood. In fact, I can't stand seafood. When I was very young, three or four years old, my mother would take me to the neighborhood market. We would stand at the seafood counter while she talked to the butcher. Under the counter was the lobster tank, right at my eye level, and I would watch the lobsters sitting in the sand at the bottom of the tank, waving their claws. To me, they were sea monsters itching to get out of the tank and get those claws on me. I was terrified, wanting to get out of there but not wanting to act like a baby about it. There was a strong smell of fish in the air, and of course I connected the two. The taste and smell of fish turn my stomach to this day.

That is one of my earliest memories. I had forgotten all about it until it came back to me years later, as an adult. There are other memories, associations even earlier than that, buried deep in my subconscious. They're still guiding me through life. I like this, and I don't like that. Most of the time, I have no idea why.

Seafood is not good and not bad. Well, it's nutritious, so that's good. And the mercury content is a concern, so that's bad. But the taste is just what it is. It's not good or bad. I don't like it, that's all.

We put labels on all our experiences. We think of them as good or bad based largely on things that happened deep in the past that we don't even remember. And we live our lives according to those labels. But the labels aren't who we really are. They're just distractions that keep us from taking the world as it really is and from seeing ourselves as we really are. There's more to us than our likes and dislikes—our labels.

We do the same with the people we meet. We're always judging others. People get in the cab, and we have them summed up in seconds. Most of the time, our judgments are based on very little. We don't like the way someone dresses, the way he steps out a little into the street as he flags down the cab, the way he slams the door when he gets in. He says something and we take it the wrong way, or we just don't like his tone of voice. Maybe we're just in a bad mood, so we assume the worst. Or we're in a great mood, so whoever gets in the cab seems pretty nice, no matter how they're dressed or how they talk. The truth is, we have no idea what they're really like unless we get to know them. And even then, our opinions say more about our moods and our preconceptions than about them. Or about us, as we really are inside.

Like most people, I have an opinion about everything. Luckily, I'm right about all of it. I'm sure that some of the opinions I held in the past must have been wrong, but I can't think of any. I thought I was wrong about something once, but I was wrong about that.

It's all right to have opinions, likes, and dislikes. We have to use our judgment as best we can to live in this world. We have to decide what to do, how to live. There's nothing wrong with enjoying one kind of music and not another. Or preferring a bacon cheeseburger over a dish of smoked salmon. And if we're going to make this world a better place, we have to form some opinions about the world and then act on them. But we get attached to our opinions the way we get attached to our other possessions. I've seen drivers ready to throw punches over which car is better for cabdriving—the Ford Crown Vic or the Chevrolet Impala.

In Zen there's a koan: what was your original face, the face you had before you were born? Meaning, what is your true nature, the nature you had before you began to pile up experiences and opinions, likes and dislikes? Before you were molded into the person you are today? Where did that true nature go? The answer is that it's still there, deep inside, covered by concepts and opinions. That is Buddha nature. *Tathagata*. Big mind. Beginner's mind. Call it the soul, if you want to. Zen practice is a process of seeing through all those things that are only temporary and learning to sense the world around you with clear eyes and an open mind. Seeing the world as it really is, without a filter of delusions and preconceptions. And learning to see yourself the same way.

Of course, Zen is not a way of erasing our personalities. Our likes and dislikes will stay with us throughout our lives. So will our other personal qualities, both "good" and "bad." Some of the great Zen masters have been temperamental and difficult, while others have been cheerful and easily approachable. We all have our unique points of view. That never changes. But the temperamental Zen master knows he is temperamental. He is aware of this. He probably even laughs at himself on occasion. He knows it's just his "monkey mind," a cloud passing over the light of his true self.

CLEAN-UP TIME

In the morning, I'm moving around the house, getting ready for the day. I'm feeling sharp, open, refreshed from zazen. I'm looking forward to getting out there, taking on that world. On the way to the door, I stumble over a pizza box that's lying on the living room floor.

I'm trying to remember when I had pizza. It's been awhile.

The living room floor is littered with food wrappers, newspapers. There are clothes strewn around the bedroom. The kitchen doesn't look too bad, but that's because I never really cook anything. There's junk mail piled on the table, a little dent in the pile where I set my morning cup of coffee. Everywhere I look there's something I should have thrown away or wiped up, but didn't. And there's dust everywhere, including on top of the clutter. I live on a dirt road near the railroad tracks, so there's plenty of dust.

If Martha Stewart came in here, she'd have a psychotic break right on the living room floor, between the pizza boxes and the burger bags. But don't worry about Martha—she won't be coming over.

It's all right, I have an excuse for the bad housekeeping. I'm working ninety hours a week. I don't have time to keep the place clean.

The fact is, I've never been much for housekeeping. I just never cared about it. I clean it up when it gets bad enough, or if someone is coming over, but I personally don't care if I can see my reflection in the juice glasses. I have a mirror for that.

I know it's time to deal with it. Not today, because it's ten forty and I have to get over to the company for checkout. But soon.

Part of Zen practice is to simplify your life, to establish simple routines and carry out those routines mindfully. Sweeping the floor or taking out the trash should be just routines. Done this way, they don't pile up, cause problems later on.

Living that way, we cut away the things that don't matter, the things that just clutter up our lives. That's hard for me to do. I tend to focus on things that really need to be done right away and save the rest for another time. You could say I over-prioritize. And I procrastinate on things that don't seem important at the moment. Like dusting. I don't really care about dust, so I leave it for later. I also make simple tasks into major, life-altering projects that I don't even remotely have time for. Instead of cutting back some of the bamboo in the back yard, I'll start planning a huge landscaping project, complete with a nice Zen waterfall in the back yard, fed by a cistern that collects rainwater and filters it . . . You get the idea.

Another problem is that I'm a pack rat. I tend to throw things into the storage shed, thinking I might want them someday. The storage shed has boxes piled up that I haven't even looked at in years. There's a broken lawn mower I thought I was going to fix, but I don't really have a lawn. There's an old air conditioner that blew a fan motor and just died. There are books I bought years ago, thinking I'd really like to know about Native American culture or chaos theory. And I would like to know about those things, but not enough to actually read four-hundred-page books about them while I'm sitting at the airport. I know the storage shed isn't really full of treasures, but I don't seem to be throwing any of it away either. Maybe there's some attachment going on.

Ironically, when there's something I really want to find, I can never find it.

My life is full of this kind of clutter. There's more to it than pizza boxes, broken equipment, and unread books. Those things are just symptoms of something deeper. You could say I have some issues, and it's hard to let them go. I know I should, and I try, but it's hard to do. We all have baggage, and we all carry some of it around. Letting go can be hard, but it's hard to make much progress when we're hanging on to the past.

I step outside and notice that the weeds are starting to take over the front yard. I've been putting that off too. What I should be doing is spending five or ten minutes each morning with the hedge clippers, cutting back the weeds one section at a time. It's not that hard. When that's done, I could do a little raking, get everything into one pile, let it turn into mulch. Then I could start in on the back yard, cut back the bamboo. Really, it's not a big yard. I should be able to keep it neat. And I will. Not today, because now it's ten forty-five and I need to get going. But soon.

All this is just a metaphor. Well, not all of it—the house really is a mess. Suzuki-roshi says that when we practice, we should have a general housecleaning of our minds. We should take everything outside, clean it up, and see whether we really need it. If not, we should just throw it away. If it is something we need, we can bring it back inside and take care of it. Taking out the mental trash and cutting back the mind weeds are important parts of Zen practice. Suzuki-roshi also says that we should be thankful for mind weeds. Dealing with the weeds nourishes the plant. Being alert, mindful, watching out for the clutter and the weeds, we learn about ourselves and get closer to understanding our true nature. Besides, if we didn't have all these metaphorical weeds and clutter to deal with, we'd just be driving around with not much to do.

Part of clearing away clutter is to avoid creating more of it. In Zen practice, everything is simplified. In the zendo, everyone wears black. It's not distracting for others, and it doesn't draw attention. No one in the zendo worries about how her clothes look. Buddhists also tend to have their heads shaved, or at least keep their hair cut short. Zen is a spiritual journey, not a fashion show.

This isn't only a Zen idea. The philosopher Ludwig Wittgenstein had his entire closet filled with identical black suits, white shirts, and black ties. He thought big thoughts. He didn't want to waste any of his energy on deciding what to wear, so he just wore the same thing every day. I can't decide if that's Zen or insanity. Maybe it's a little of both.

In the zendo, everyone speaks quietly, mostly about practice, if they speak at all. There really isn't much to say in a zendo. Most of what we talk about in day-to-day life seems trivial in that setting. Meals are simple. The point isn't to create a gourmet meal, but to enjoy the simple food as it is.

Zendos are also very neatly kept.

I need a general housecleaning of the mind, just like Suzuki-roshi says. I need to take out everything that weighs on me, take a good look at it, and make a decision. Is this something that is relevant to the life I live today? Is this something I can use? Or is it just useless crap that weighs me down? My guess is that I'd be amazed at just how much I can do without.

That's what I'm doing, a little at a time. That's what Zen is about. Sitting on my cushion in the morning, thoughts come up and fade away. Most of them are just clutter, and I let them go. Some of them seem to come up a lot. But really, they're just junk mail on the kitchen table, weeds overrunning the flowers. I don't need them. And over time, I realize that most of the thoughts that come up—and not just in zazen—are only clutter. Maybe, in a way, all of them are.

One of the advantages of cabdriving is that it forces you to clean up the clutter in your life. Working these hours, having to focus on what you're doing, you just forget about whole stretches of your life. Then when you think of them, you realize they weren't as important as you thought they were. And you might find that you really cared about some of it, and you can focus on that instead. There's a balance to maintain. Simplifying your life doesn't mean getting rid of it entirely. Life should be simple and uncluttered, not empty.

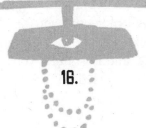

FISHING THE MOONLIGHT

In life, it's important to have goals. They give us direction and motivation. When I pick up a fare, the first thing I say is, "Where would you like to go?" Now there's a goal, a destination. I know where I'm going. I take a moment to consider the best route. Then I stop thinking about the destination and start driving.

In Zen, the goal is to attain spiritual growth that may lead to enlightenment. But the goal is put aside in the actual practice. Goals are something extra. They distract us from living mindfully. Zen is about living in the moment, doing that from moment to moment throughout the day. Then doing it the next day, and the day after that. Zen is about the process of living, not the result.

Keep your eyes on the prize, they say. They're wrong. That's bad advice for cabdrivers and bodhisattvas alike. If you keep your eyes on the prize, you won't be focused on the step you're taking right now, and that step is the one that counts. Keep your eyes on the prize and you'll stumble. Or drive into a telephone pole. Keep your eyes on the road.

In cabdriving, there's a simple goal. Book as many fares for as much money as you can before you wear down. Then come back the next day and do that again. It sounds simple, and it is. But if you're thinking about that, you won't get much driving done.

Once you know what the goal is, you can stop thinking about it and focus on the hour-to-hour, minute-to-minute, instant-to-instant tasks that lead to the goal. The goal of getting your passengers to their destinations and the goal of being productive as a cabdriver are really the same goal. Both go step by step. And most of the steps are the same. Knowing this, you can follow them mindfully, without being distracted by a goal.

That's how Zen works.

Each morning while I drink my first cup of coffee, I figure up the money from the day before. I add up the fares from my trip sheet (tips included) and subtract the day's lease, gasoline, and car wash expenses. That's my net for the day, my score. Not only does the score sum up what I did that day, it says a lot about the way I did it. Today my score is 49. It doesn't sound like much for a twelve-hour shift, but that's for a Monday, so it's not so bad. I'll do better on the weekend.

It's a score; it's not money. It's not something to get attached to. In my mind, it's as if I played a round of golf yesterday and made a score. The score sums up the way I played over the eighteen holes, but it's only a score. There is more to golf, or cabdriving, than that.

I'm reading an essay by Taisen Deshimaru, a Soto Zen master who taught in Europe for fifteen years before his death in 1982. Deshimaru is one of my favorites. His writing is dramatic, mysterious. It's fun to read, even when it's incomprehensible. And often, it is. The essay is titled "Mushotoku: No Goal or Desire for Gain." It's about avoiding attachment to wisdom or attainment. In it, he says that avoiding attachment to wisdom is itself the greatest wisdom. I read it twice (Deshimaru's essays are mercifully short, just right for cabstand reading) and start in again. It begins: "Having even one goal, even the tiniest preference or the most infinitesimal thought, or pursuing some objective, however feeble, automatically and inevitably drives us away from the truth of Zazen."

Cabdrivers are pretty tough-minded when it comes to goals. The daily total—the score—is a point of pride for the drivers. It's also an effective motivational tool. Working twelve to fifteen hours in a shift, it's easy to slack off, get distracted. When that happens, the day can get away quickly. There's not much worse than putting in a twelve-hour shift and winding up with only enough money to cover expenses. And it happens. Keeping a running total for the day helps prevent it.

Cabdrivers have slumps like anyone else. Sometimes the edge is just gone. You find yourself spending too much time in line at the airport, sitting around a parking lot drinking coffee, waiting for something to happen. It takes a real effort to break out of it. You can self-actualize or visualize success or choose your destiny. You can be a samurai cabdriver, a warrior behind the wheel. You can channel Steve McQueen. You can use a word—*relentless*, for example—as a mantra to push yourself to excel. Whatever works.

Or you can focus on your goal. Your score. Sometimes you just have to think about your score as you go about your day. It's a way of reminding yourself why you're out there. Most days, I know exactly what my score is without even wanting to, just out of habit. Every time I drop someone off, I add the fare to the running total. I don't try, it just happens. Sometimes, when I need to, I use it to push myself. Eighty dollars. Seven o'clock. Not good enough. I have to do better.

But that's not real cabdriving. That's a distraction. Cabdriving is about handling the car, figuring the routes, flowing through the traffic, dealing with the passengers. It's about being sharp and focused in your driving. You have to take things as they come and deal with them, and then let them go. Visualizing success and keeping score are extra, just more distractions from the real work.

That's Zen. Taking life a moment at a time, living it, and then letting it go. Everything else is a distraction. A score is a distraction. A goal is a distraction.

There are goals in Zen practice. Steps along the path that have to be taken. We are trying to develop personal qualities that will help us on the path. We are trying to master the precepts. We are deepening our meditation practice, bringing more mindfulness to our everyday lives. It doesn't happen all at once. We resolve to be more patient, and in time, we find that happening. We have to be aware of our progress, and when we stall out, we have to recognize that and take steps to do better. While goals are hard to define—and benchmarks don't really exist at all—we can focus on the simple goal of making steady progress. And we can dedicate ourselves to doing that every day.

While we're doing this, we have to live in the real world. And the world is part of our practice. We might think that Zen practice will help us to be more effective in our personal or professional lives. We might even think it will help us to be better cabdrivers. If these goals help us to maintain an active practice, that's good, but the goals aren't important in themselves. This is not a self-help program. This is not *Mindful Motivational Methods*.

On Dharma Road, the only goal that really matters is the quest for enlightenment. And that can be the greatest distraction of all. We can't think too much about enlightenment. It's a long way off. This moment is the only moment that matters. To attain our goals, we need to have no goals at all. As Seung Sahn puts it, "Wanting enlightenment is a big mistake."

I'm reading another of Deshimaru's essays, "Penetrate Our True Nature." In it he says, "Sitting in Zazen is like fishing the moonlight and plowing the clouds. The mind opens wide, everything grows calm, you can become close to yourself." That's what I want in this life, to fish the moonlight. To plow the clouds. This is a world of mystery and wonder, and I want to be part of that. I want my mind to open wide, and wherever that leads, that's where I want to go.

I don't need a goal for that. I don't need to keep score.

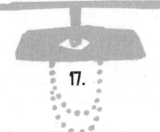

BLUE MONDAY

I'm working the downtown streets on a Monday night around ten, and there's not much to do. There's a strange feeling in the air tonight, blues notes filtering out of the clubs, a tired yellow light in the mist that hangs over the city. There's an old man with a guitar, playing for change, being drowned out by the feedback from the club on the corner. A man in a motorized wheelchair holds up flowers in a twisted hand, but the people just walk by without looking.

I pull up at the cabstand at 6th and Trinity, sitting fourth on the left side, with three other cabs across the street. I'll be here awhile. The drivers are standing around, leaning on fenders, arms folded over their chests. They're looking off into the distance, waiting for something to happen. I'm thinking, *If it's like this, I might as well be out at the airport,* but I don't want to be out there. I might as well go home, but I don't want to be there either. There's too much on my mind. I need to be doing something, but there's nothing to do right now. I get out and lean on the car, figuring I'll see what happens.

I turn the radio to "Blue Monday" on KUT, the weekly blues show, and roll down the window, let a little of the music out, just enough so I can hear it. There's a sad guitar, someone singing another song about that lonesome highway. The one that leads out of town and doesn't come back. I think it's John Lee Hooker, but I'm not sure. It seems to fit the mood tonight. It's a soundtrack for a slow night out on the street.

This is a night for reflection. You can see it in people's faces, everyone thinking about how they got here, wondering where they're going. The drivers all look like they want to get in the cabs and drive, just keep going and not look back. I feel that way myself. I feel like a guy in one of those Joe Ely songs about West Texas, a guy leaning against the fender of a cab while he waits for the storms to come in.

Of course, it's not the night at all. It's me. It's just my mood. But it feels real to me.

In Western books about spirituality, there's often a little blurb about the author's life before he set out on his own spiritual path. The author was a successful account executive with a corner office, a home in Scarsdale, an adoring family, and a Lincoln Navigator in the driveway. He had it all, but his life seemed empty somehow. You won't hear that from me.

If you want to know about emptiness, try this: Get behind the wheel of cab 119 at ten o'clock in the morning, then spend sixteen hours hustling fares, fighting traffic, and dealing with people you don't know, people you'll never see again. Try dealing with drug addicts, drunks, and self-made millionaires, all of them thinking you're a low-life creep trying to pad the meter on them. Then come home to a three-room rent house over by the Union Pacific tracks carrying a roast beef sub from Thundercloud, a carton of Nestle Quik, and a couple of scratch-off lotto tickets. Your footsteps echo from the walls, and the only other sound is the refrigerator coming on. That's emptiness.

I'm usually a pretty cheerful guy, but the truth is, there's some darkness in my life too. Maybe you noticed that already. Tonight, it's coming out a little. It's Blue Monday.

There's some of that in all our lives, if we look hard enough. I don't have to look that hard. I have regrets, moments of despair. That's all right. I deserve to have some sadness in my life, and I don't mind enduring a little pain. Maybe I have some karma to work through. I'm working on it.

Then again, what I'm doing isn't that hard. I think about Muddy Waters, Howlin' Wolf, all those other great bluesmen picking cotton all day, then playing in a beer joint at night for nickels, singing about their lives, wanting something better. I don't have it so bad.

I could be in Darfur. Or Baghdad. That would be worse.

I've read a lot of books about Buddhism. The authors traveled to Nepal at twenty, learned to speak five languages fluently, including ancient Sanskrit, and attained full enlightenment in a Himalayan cave at twenty-three. I didn't. That's all right too. I did some other things, lived the way I wanted to most of the time. I've had some good times and some bad times, like anyone. It's today that matters. We're all here right now, and the past is just a sideshow. On these streets, I'm a bodhisattva in a Hawaiian shirt and a ball cap, driving down that Eightfold Freeway in a spotless Yellow Cab, trying to get through these blues without giving in to them. We learn by overcoming our limitations, and I've got plenty of those. So I should be able to learn plenty.

The problem of suffering—and the way to ease it—is the starting point of the entire Buddhist philosophy, but it's interpreted in different ways by different schools of thought. What, really, is suffering? Is it physical and mental anguish or only our reactions to these feelings? Modern authors have presented some interesting and original versions of these ideas. For example, the Eightfold Path has traditionally been seen as leading to the end of suffering, but a modern view is that it merely helps us to deal with the suffering that is an inevitable part of our lives. This really is a debate over the definition of suffering, not the reality of it. We all suffer, but we don't have to let it dominate our lives. We don't have to attach to it.

The Buddha faced great personal tragedies in his own life. His mother died giving birth to him, a burden he carried throughout his life. His family and friends were caught up in the upheavals of their turbulant times, and often suffered harsh consequences. One of his followers, a king and a close friend, was starved to death by his own son, who wanted to take over the throne. And the son was later killed by his son. The Buddha led a large group of wandering monks and helped them deal with the problems they all faced. Late in his life, he faced old age and sickness, and finally death. Certainly, he was saddened by many of these trials. But he faced them calmly and with great compassion.

Zen practice helps us to develop a calm, even temperament that helps in the development of mindfulness in everyday life. It takes time. Along the way, there can be periods of depression and despair. We're learning about ourselves, and some of the news is bound to be hard to take. On a night like this, it takes some faith to believe that better days are ahead. But I have faith, and I'm staying on the road.

The result of this training is the Middle Way, a path that avoids the extreme emotions and the psychodramas that can cripple us in our attempts at spiritual development. For some, the Middle Way suggests an emotional distance, an isolation. They think it means to go through life oblivious to emotions. But another part of the Zen ideal is to be fully involved in our lives, and that includes the emotions that are such an important part of life. We still feel fear, sadness, anger, and the rest of the range of human emotion, but we don't dwell on any of it. We don't wallow. We don't let it pull us down. In practice, the Zen path is to avoid the overwhelming emotions that come with attachments and cravings while experiencing fully the honest, meaningful emotions that are part of a fully lived life.

A buddha is not an automaton going through life without experiencing the most basic human feelings. None of us wants to live in such a state. A buddha feels the same emotions as others, probably more deeply than most of us, but without being dominated by them. He suffers, but he doesn't wallow. He is fully aware of his emotional responses and is able to keep them in perspective. That's my understanding of the problem of suffering. Maybe someday I'll be able to explain from my own experience how a buddha deals with emotions. For now, I guess I'll just suffer along with everyone else.

Another song comes out from the radio, an old folk blues. It's Fred Neil doing "The Other Side of this Life." It suits my mood tonight: "The ten-cent life I've been leading here/Gonna be the death of me." But then comes the chorus, and there's another side to this life, and I'm standing in this cabstand seeing a way through the darkness around us, seeing some light shining through. There's a soft rain falling, the city lights shining up from the asphalt streets, people hurrying along, trying to stay dry, not really caring if they do. The cabdrivers are still out, leaning on their fenders, taking it all in. Watching the world as it is. We can take it. We can stand a little rain.

That's the blues, right there. That's life. Some sadness, with plenty of spirit. Sadness is just something else to appreciate in life. Something else to rise above. There's beauty in sadness, just as in all of life. Without a little sadness "Blue Monday" would be just another black-and-white night.

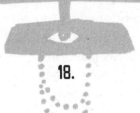

THANK YOU, THANK YOU

At the end of every ride, I say thank you to my passengers. It's just common courtesy. They pay me, maybe with a nice tip added in, and I thank them. Maybe they thank me for getting them where they were going in one piece. We always do that when money and service are involved.

"Here, keep this."

"Thank you."

"Don't mention it. Thank you."

It's all a little mechanical. We thank each other all the time, but we don't really give it much thought. Usually we don't even know what we're thanking each other for. It's just a custom. A reflex. Thank you for paying me for doing my job. Thank you for doing your job.

But it's not just about the money. We've just shared a unique experience. No matter how uneventful the ride might have been, it was a once-in-a-lifetime experience. Something we'll never get to do again. So we might say thank you for the interesting conversation. Thank you for complimenting me on my driving. Thank you for not screaming when I drifted a little into oncoming traffic. Or thank you for not shooting me. It's a cab, after all, and the bar can be set pretty low.

But we don't say any of that. We just complete the transaction and go on our way.

There's so much in life to be grateful for, but we don't think about that. We should be saying thank you all the time. We should be thanking each other, and we should be thanking the world around us. After all, if we were really on our own, we wouldn't last long. But we don't do that. We're always focused on what we want and what we don't have and we forget to be grateful for what we have. That's grasping. That's attachment. That's human nature, but it doesn't help us to be more human.

Gratitude is the opposite of attachment. Instead of grasping for what we lack, we should take a good look at what we have and be thankful for that. Even if we don't have much. In Buddhism, the greatest gift is this human life. We could have been reborn as armadillos. Or hungry ghosts. Instead we get to live a human life. We should always remember to be grateful for that. If we are alive and we have a stone to sit on and air to breathe, we can sit in zazen and learn to see deep within ourselves to our true human nature. We should be thankful for life, a stone, and the air. Everything else is just a wonderful bonus.

Most of us have much more than the bare necessities. A Mahayana Buddhist practice is to make a list of everything we are given in the course of a day—not cab fares, but the small blessings that come our way. A tasty snack. A song on the radio. A water cooler with really cold water. They add up. If we keep a list, we can look back at the end of the day and realize just how lucky we are. And we can be thankful for that.

Much of Zen practice is just to develop an appreciation for everyday life. Whether it's a glorious sunrise over the green hills of Texas or a frantic street scene anywhere in the world, we should take it all in and see the beauty behind it. And we can appreciate that and give thanks for it. Wherever we are, we're lucky to be there. We're lucky just to be.

But it's easy to be thankful for small blessings and sunrises. We only have to notice them. The hard times are valuable as well. They say what doesn't kill you makes you stronger, and some of us ought to be pretty strong by now. We can be grateful for the trials we face, the obstacles we have to overcome. They will help us to grow. We have to remember that when the times get hard. We have to be mindful, to appreciate our lives.

Years ago, I knew some reggae musicians. Many of them were devout Rastas. One night, some of them were on their way home from a gig when their van was involved in a serious accident. The van was on its side, wrecked, their equipment scattered around the street. Some of them were injured. They sat together on the pavement while they waited for the ambulance and prayed, giving thanks to Ja. Someone asked them later why they would be thankful in that moment.

"We were alive," one of them said. The others smiled, nodded.

We're alive too. We should all give thanks.

Who should we thank for our good fortune? Ja? God? Allah? Buddha? The Goddess? The Great Spirit? Or just this amazing world that sustains us? It doesn't matter. The Great Spirit doesn't need our thanks. The world is just the world. The point is simply to remind ourselves how lucky we are to have these human lives. And how important it is not to waste them.

Bowing is a spiritual practice all around the world. Muslims make a daily practice of bowing in the direction of Mecca. Christian ceremonies include bowing and kneeling. In the East, bowing is part of everyday manners as well as an expression of religious reverence. A Korean Zen practice is to bow 1,080 times during the day. The bows express our gratitude for our precious lives and everything we have to fill them with. Mainly, they remind us of our good fortune.

It's customary to bow after doing zazen. It could be one bow, three, or nine. Or any other number. The point is to do it mindfully. It's not an empty ritual. It's not a way to loosen up the back before standing. Or a way to end the session gracefully. Each bow is a letting go of the ego, the small, deluded mind. It is a reminder that we are only small parts of something much larger. Each bow is a way of saying thanks.

Suzuki-roshi always stressed the importance of bowing, making it a central part of his students' practice. He told of his own teacher, who had a callus on his forehead from bowing. His teacher had been stubborn and difficult when he was younger, and he'd emphasized bowing in his practice as a way to overcome this. Some of us should be bowing enough to turn our foreheads black and blue. I know I should.

And by the way, since we're on the subject, thank you for reading *Dharma Road*. It might seem like something

I ran off in the cab during a long wait in the airport line, but the truth is I put a lot of time and effort into it. And a lot of myself. It means a lot to me that anyone would take enough of an interest to read it.

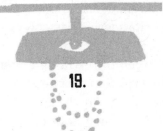

THE RIGHT LIFE

There's some irony in the idea of a cabdriver giving advice about ethics. One of the worst things about driving a cab is that so many people believe we are basically crooks. Comedians are always cracking jokes about cabdrivers. David Letterman has a lot to answer for on this. If I ever meet him, we'll have a talk. I've had lobbyists, lawyers, stockbrokers, and politicians in the cab telling me not to run up the meter, they know their way around. People think we're always trying to pull one hustle or another, but it's usually not true. Usually. Most of the drivers are honest, hardworking people who get more upset about the few dishonest drivers than the passengers do. And the really crooked drivers get booted out on their butts before very long.

There was a driver a few years back who figured out that the waiting time on the meter kicked in any time the cab's speed dropped below nine miles an hour, charging the passenger for both time and distance. He started driving under nine as often as he could get away with it, turning eight dollar fares into twenty dollar epic journeys and irritating his passengers no end. Which might sound pretty clever, except for two small problems. First, between the extra time spent on each fare and the fact that he didn't get any tips at all, he didn't make any extra money. And he got so many complaints that he got fired in a matter of days. In the long run, stealing doesn't pay, even in the cab business. But sometimes it's a really long run.

There's a stunt called waterhauling that some of the drivers pull. When the dispatcher assigns a call to a driver, the other drivers hear about it on the radio, and they're supposed to stay away from that block until the call's been loaded. But sometimes a driver will decide he's close enough to load the other driver's fare and get away before he shows up. This happens most often to rookie drivers who get a reputation for taking too long to cover their calls. Waterhauling leads to some real bad blood between drivers, not to mention bad driving and an occasional fistfight. Sometimes a driver gets a reputation for it and becomes a target for the others. I've seen waterhaulers driven out of the cab business permanently. Good riddance.

It's like Bob Dylan said, "To live outside the law"—or just off on the margins where things are more interesting—"you must be honest." Most drivers figure that one out pretty quickly.

Ethical and moral standards in Buddhism are defined by two sets of precepts, one general, the other more specific. They are an extension of right action, the fourth step on the Eightfold Path. In formal Zen practice, there is a ritual in which a student takes a solemn vow to live according to the precepts. I haven't taken a formal vow—I'm a pretty informal kind of guy, not much for ritual—but I do my best to follow the spirit of the precepts. It doesn't take a formal vow to commit to living an ethical, moral life.

The Three Collective Pure Precepts are:

1. Avoid all that is evil.
2. Practice all that is good.
3. Purify the mind.

This is simply a general statement of what it means to practice Buddhism. It's a little vague. Good and evil are not defined in these precepts. They relate to actions that strengthen or weaken the practice, not to some detailed moral code. When we have a clear conscience, practice becomes easier and our lives are fuller. Then we can purify the mind.

Good and evil are subjective: we should know the difference intuitively. And usually, we do. Unfortunately, sometimes we manage to delude ourselves into doing something we want to do even though we know it's wrong. A psychologist would call this rationalization. Alcoholics are great at this. A drinker might celebrate that first week of sobriety with a drink, telling himself he's earned it. We all find excuses to do what we want, even when we know better. By purifying the mind, we can avoid the self-deceptions that trip us up. Purifying the mind means to practice meditation and mindfulness diligently, without becoming distracted.

The Ten Grave Precepts are more specific. They prohibit actions that will cause serious difficulties for us. In their original form, there were only five, but some years after the Buddha passed on, someone decided ten was a more pleasing number than five, and five more precepts were added to make the list complete. The result is what I like to call the Five Really Grave Precepts and the Five Moderately Important Precepts.

The Ten Grave Precepts are:

1. No killing.
2. No stealing.
3. No misuse of sex.
4. No lying.
5. No use of drugs.
6. No speaking ill of others.
7. No praising of self.
8. No sparing of dharma assets.
9. No indulgence in anger.
10. No slandering the Three Treasures.

The form of the precepts makes them seem a little like the Ten Commandments, but they are very different. While the commandments are a set of specific rules (Thou shalt not . . .) handed down from God, the precepts really describe the conduct of an enlightened being, a buddha. A buddha, for example, would never kill another being, or even think about doing it. A buddha would have compassion for all beings. Those who wish to become buddhas will show compassion and avoid killing. Sometimes the precept is expressed in the form "There is no killing," meaning that in the mind of an enlightened being, killing just doesn't exist. It's unthinkable. The punishment for violating the precepts is only that the weight of one's actions leads to distraction and creates bad karma in this and future lives, making it more difficult to attain enlightenment.

It's like the Christians say: "Act as if you have faith and faith will be granted to you." If you live as a buddha lives, you might just become a buddha.

The precepts serve as the starting point for an ethical system that is deeply subjective. For example, the First Precept, no killing, can be interpreted narrowly as prohibiting only the killing of other people. It is also interpreted by many Buddhists (not all) as prohibiting the killing of any animals and the eating of meat, since animals must be killed to provide the meat. It also may prohibit the killing of pest insects, such as fire ants and fleas. In extreme cases, some sects have filtered their drinking water to remove the microorganisms that would otherwise be killed when swallowed. The exact interpretation of the precepts is an individual matter.

Personally, I'm not going to strain my water for microbes. And when it comes to fire ants and fleas, DDT is too good for the sons of . . . In Texas, the cockroaches are two inches long. With wings. Compassion for insects isn't a priority around here. But that's just my own opinion. I'm pretty sure Buddha never taught anything like that. And he never used insecticides. Maybe in time, I'll learn to take a wider view. Or I'll move someplace where the insects are more likable.

The Second Precept prohibits stealing. This applies not only to pickpocketing, armed robbery, and padding the taxi meter, but to more subtle forms of theft, such as the destruction of the environment and the exploitation of others. Attitude is important: attachment to possessions is at the heart of all forms of stealing, and attachment is not the way to enlightenment.

The Third Precept prohibits the misuse of sex. Sex is not prohibited outside of monastic practice, and misuse of sex is not defined by the precept. Is sex between unmarried people allowed? How about gay and lesbian sex? How about . . . uh, never mind. This isn't *Taxicab Confessions*. The precepts have been interpreted in many ways, but in the end, we all have to reach our own understanding and live by that. One suggestion: if you think you're misusing sex, you probably are.

The Fourth Precept prohibits lying. Truth is central to Buddhism; the point of practice is to learn to see ourselves as we truly are. To learn the truth and face it squarely. To deny the truth is to deny the practice. Lies of all kinds are therefore prohibited. Like the other precepts, however, it's a matter of interpretation. Some of those little white lies don't seem so bad. (By the way, you look very nice today.) And in situations where lying will prevent a greater harm, it might be acceptable. But again, if you think you're lying, you are. And if you're not sure, you probably shouldn't be talking.

The Fifth Precept bans the use of drugs. Originally, this was meant only as a ban on alcohol, but there are a lot of drugs around today that were unknown in ancient India. All mood-enhancing drugs—marijuana, heroin, cocaine, psilocybin, amphetamines, ecstasy, and whatever else they're coming up with today—interfere with spiritual growth and should be avoided. Some people need prescription drugs for such problems as depression or anxiety disorders. Again, these are all personal decisions. Medical marijuana would probably be all right, if it's really medical. In a commentary by Zen master Robert Aitken, he suggests that indulging in diversions such as television is another type of drug use and should also be avoided.

The other five precepts are also important, but they are either very general or they relate to the practice itself and don't come up in everyday life. They ban criticizing, bragging, getting mad, and being selfish. These are pretty obvious. It's best not to praise yourself or to criticize others, and most of what happens when we indulge in anger just leads to more trouble. Trust me. I know about that one. Avoiding selfishness really means to help others, particularly in a spiritual setting.

The Tenth Precept, no slandering the Three Treasures, is really trivial. The Three Treasures—Buddha, Dharma, and Sangha (spiritual community)—are the whole of Buddhist practice. Anyone who would violate this precept would no doubt have driven off the dharma bridge long ago. Apparently the ancestors had some trouble coming up with a tenth precept, but they liked the number so they just phoned this one in.

Mindfulness is the key to practicing the precepts. It's one thing to read about them, but out in the real world, living by them can be a challenge. I've always seen myself as an honest, ethical person, but sometimes I've been deluded, weak, self-absorbed. Hard to believe, I know, but it's true. Looking back, I know I've done things that were destructive to myself and others. I always meant well, tried to do the right thing. I never meant to do any harm, but I'm not perfect. I'm making more of an effort now, keeping an active awareness of the precepts, trying to see how my actions affect the course of my life and the lives around me.

But it's only an effort. Maybe a true buddha can see the twists of karma and the turns of self-delusion clearly, but for the rest of us, it's still mostly a mystery. We're all works in progress, and all we can do is try to do a little better today and a little better than that tomorrow. And maybe that will be enough.

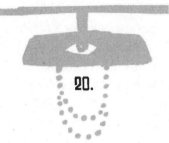

LOVING LOVING-KINDNESS

Driving a cab, you meet a lot of people. In a typical twelve-hour shift, a driver will load twenty fares, about thirty or forty people in all, and spend about fifteen minutes with them. You talk about the weather, sports, good places to eat, what's going on this weekend. You don't talk about politics. Or religion. You don't get to know any of these people. It's all pretty impersonal. You just pick them up and drop them off, and you never see them again.

This gives us a great opportunity to have a positive—or negative—effect on the lives of people without being drawn into the ongoing psychodramas that can turn day-to-day life into such an emotional minefield. For drivers on the Eightfold Freeway, this is where right action comes into play. This is where the Golden Rule rules.

The Buddha taught compassion for all beings. In Buddhism, compassion is generally thought of as an active feeling of empathy, a willingness to share in the suffering of others. It grows from the realization that we are not really separate from each other. We are all parts of a much greater pattern. In other words, we're all in this together. To hurt others is to hurt ourselves. And in daily life, that's not just a saying. It's reality.

Compassion and empathy are central to all religions. In Christianity, there is a great emphasis on the practice of forgiveness. When Pope John Paul II forgave the man who shot and nearly killed him, it was a great spiritual lesson for the world. And the selflessness of such leaders as Mother Teresa and the Dalai Lama is an inspiration for people of all faiths.

Right action means to have compassion for all beings, not just the ones who deserve it. The bad drivers, the self-absorbed creeps, the road ragers, the crackheads—they'll all pay a heavy price for their actions. The toxic passengers will run into real trouble down the line. They're looking for it, and they'll find it. There's suffering in their lives as well. We don't need to add to it. And we don't have to add to anyone else's burdens either.

It's hard making a living behind the wheel of a cab. The drivers have to hustle long hours and handle a heavy load of stress to make it all pay. That can seem like a good excuse to act out. It's not. We're always better off when we're helping others.

I'm at the airport, second up at the cabstand in front of the terminal. I've been waiting in line for almost two hours, and I just want to get going. In front of me is a driver named Ray who always works the airport. He's standing at the back of his cab with the trunk open, a vacant smile on his face. He looks at me, shrugs, looks back at the terminal, fidgets a little. He's watching the stragglers from the previous flights, people who've been using the restrooms, waiting for luggage. They're coming out a few at a time, mostly heading for the parking lots.

I know what he's thinking. He's watching the people as they come out, trying to guess which ones want a cab, how far they'll be going. Some of the drivers have the variables all worked out: the number of people in a group, the way they're dressed, the amount and type of luggage, a long list of factors. Sometimes they'll stand there in the cab line, debating the possibilities, arguing about the people coming out. Sometimes they even bet on it. Ray's thinking about it now, deciding which ones he wants, which he doesn't. He's been in line for a long time, and he's been thinking about the big fare he's going to get, getting attached to the idea of it. He thinks he deserves a good one just for waiting. Not that it matters. Whoever comes out next and wants a cab, that's who he's getting.

It takes a few minutes. Then a woman comes up, in her fifties, well-dressed, trailing an overnight bag on wheels. I'm thinking she's going to a hotel, probably downtown, not a long trip. He's thinking the same but he keeps the smile on, says hello. He picks up the bag, puts it in the trunk, and I can read his lips as he says, "Where would you like to go?"

Apparently, he doesn't like the answer. The smile drops away. He reaches up, slams the trunk. Walks around the car with his lips moving, a nasty look on his face. Pounds a fist into the roof as he opens the door and gets in. The poor woman is still standing there, at the back of the cab, looking shocked. She's wondering what she did wrong. She's probably wondering if she should get in the cab with this guy. He might be dangerous. Or crazy. Finally, she goes around, opens the door, and gets in.

Welcome to Austin, ma'am. Enjoy your stay.

Familiar, isn't it? We get so wrapped up in ourselves that we lose all connection with the people around us. It happens all the time. I know Ray a little, and he's got some issues. He's actually a pretty nice guy, but he keeps to himself most of the time. He's a little on edge. And, like most of us, he didn't see himself sitting in the cab line at the airport when he graduated from high school.

Part of living the dharma is connecting with other people. Seeing the connections that unite us. It's hard to do sometimes. Out on the streets, it's a hard life, and that makes for a great excuse. It's easy to just look out for number one.

This teaching of compassion is one of the cornerstones of all Buddhist practices. In Mahayana Buddhism, compassion is expressed as part of the bodhisattva ideal of living for the benefit of all beings. The practice of Tonglen involves taking on the suffering of others in a very real way. For some schools, compassion is the main focus of the practice. One school, called Vipassana, or Insight Meditation, emphasizes the development of compassion through rigorous introspection. This practice is called metta, or loving-kindness. Loving-kindness—all one word, said with a soft, hopeful smile.

The practice of loving-kindness includes meditations aimed at the development of personal qualities such as serenity and a sense of personal safety that lead in turn to a great compassion for others. For example, we might chant, "May I be safe from physical harm," over and over, like a mantra. With sufficient practice, we attain a feeling of safety and personal security. Once that is achieved, it's easier to be open to the needs of others.

It seems like a lot of work. After all, the point is simply to be a decent human being. That doesn't seem so hard. But these are difficult times, and it's easy to find excuses to let this aspect of our practice slide. We have to take care of ourselves, and we may not have much left over for others.

Loving-kindness doesn't come easy to me, which probably means I should take it up and work extra hard on it. There's a book on the Buddhist shelf at the library, *Gentling the Heart*. When I see the title, I know it's not for me. People who would want to read a book like that probably don't need to be that much more loving toward others. And the people who need it the most—like me, or Ray, out at the airport—won't read it.

You don't see much loving-kindness out on the streets these days. Everyone's battling the traffic, trying to get ahead of everyone else. We could use a few real bodhisattvas out here. People who can help calm things down and show the rest of us how it could be. I'd like to do that myself, but I've got a ways to go. I'm working on it. And I'm learning.

I pull up at the Greyhound station on a Tuesday afternoon, second in the cab line. Business is bad, even for a Tuesday. Midsummer in Austin. It's been slow for weeks. People with money are all vacationing somewhere that's cooler than the surface of the sun. The rest of us are stuck here chasing dollars. There's nothing coming out on the cab radio. I'd go out to the airport and sit in line there, but that hasn't been turning over either. Besides, this is closer. I keep the air conditioner running, engine on, burning gas.

Nothing happens at the bus station until a bus comes in, and there aren't that many buses. Drivers who work it regularly know the schedule. I don't. I figure I'll just sit there until something happens. I might get a long fare, something to make my afternoon. Some good fares come out of the bus station. Or I might wait two hours for a five-dollar ride. It seems like the best of a long list of bad bets.

I've got those midsummer cabdriver blues. I've got 'em bad.

After a while, I shut off the engine and get out. I'd sit in the shade, but there isn't any. I walk over to the back of the station, where the buses load. There are a few people on the benches there, waiting for the next bus. They all look like they're going to nod off or dissolve in the sun. I'd go inside and check the schedule, which would be the smart thing to do, but I don't want to know.

There's a woman at the back of the station with a little girl. They look lost. She loads some suitcases and a taped cardboard box onto a small cart and sits the girl on top, pushes the cart out to the sidewalk. The girl enjoys the ride, but it's a short one. The woman stands there looking around.

They don't look like they can afford a cab.

Finally she takes the girl by the hand and walks over. "Excuse me, do you know where the Salvation Army is located?"

It's downtown, four or five miles from the bus station. I tell her that.

She looks troubled. The little girl is looking at her reflection in the door of the cab. She can't see much, but she seems entranced. In this heat, she'll be wailing soon enough. The woman thinks it over and asks, "Where can I catch a bus?"

If I were king of the world, or just the head of Capitol Metro, I would put a bus stop right next to the Greyhound station. After all, it is a bus station. But there isn't a stop anywhere near here. I start describing the route she'll have to take to the closest bus stop, which is at Highland Mall. I glance over at the suitcases, the cardboard box sealed with duct tape. I look at the woman. She looks like she has a black eye. Not a bad one, but it's there. I can't do this.

"Come on, I'll give you a ride over there."

"Are you sure? I can't afford to pay you. I know you have to make a living out here."

"It's all right. I'm not exactly getting rich sitting here." I walk over and collect the cart with the suitcases and the box, wheel it over to the cab. I load the trunk. The little girl stands on her toes on the curb, studying the inside of the trunk.

I'm thinking I'm going to give her a ride to the bus stop, then get back in line at the station, but I'm picturing her trying to get the suitcases on a city bus. I make a turn and head for the interstate, downtown. I feel better already. I crank up the air conditioner.

On the way in, we talk. It's what I thought. She was in an abusive relationship, and she's getting out. She's here to start over. She asks if all the people in Austin are as nice as I am, and I tell her, yes, most of them are, but I'm not usually this nice. I'm working on it.

When we get to the Salvation Army, I help her with her bags. The people there are expecting her. She won't be staying at the shelter. They're going to help her get a new start. As I turn to leave, the little girl looks up at me, gives me a beautiful smile, and says thank you. It's the first thing she's said since she left the back of the bus station. It's like the sun coming out on a dark afternoon.

From there, I head over to the Omni and load a fifty-dollar fare to Georgetown, and while I'm there, a call comes out on the radio and I load another coming all the way back downtown and then . . .

No. Of course not. Life isn't like that. It's still a Tuesday afternoon in July. I pull up third in line at the Omni and wait there an hour to load a five-dollar fare going over to the capitol. But I feel good about it. That's what counts.

And a week from now, when I look back at what I've been doing, I'll realize that that was the best afternoon of my week. That was the one time I felt like I belonged in this world, like I had something real and important to do in this life.

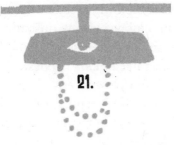

LISTEN TO THIS

I'm out in the cab on a Thursday afternoon, working the radio calls, trying to keep the fares turning over. I take a call at Barton Creek Square Mall. It's a middle-aged woman in a gaudy green pants suit. She's carrying a couple bags, and when she gets in, she tells me she wants to go to Circle C. That's a subdivision south of Austin, pretty much a straight shot down Mopac.

"Yes, ma'am," I say, cheerfully. "Have a nice time shopping today?"

"Yes, I had a great time. I had to get some new clothes for this weekend. My daughter is coming up for the weekend with her husband, they live down in Schertz—that's outside San Antonio, he works for Southwestern Bell, well I guess it's AT&T now, he's a supervisor down there. She's a teacher, second grade, she's great with kids, a natural. Anyway, they're coming up for the weekend, and we're going out to a real fancy restaurant, the four of us, them and me and my husband. I don't know which restaurant we're going to, but something real nice, and

I wanted to get something nice to wear because I don't get to go out much because my husband doesn't really like to do that, so we usually stay in, so when I get to go somewhere nice, I like to look my best. . . ."

Actually, I'm not following any of this. I'm not listening. I'd like to say I'm focusing on my driving, practicing the mindful way of motoring, but it's just a simple drive down Mopac, not much traffic down here in the early afternoon, so there's not much to focus on. I'm just not interested in what she's saying. I don't care what her son-in-law does, unless he drives a cab down there. Then I might get interested. Or he's a Zen master. That would get my attention.

I'm doing what we all do in this situation. I'm hearing enough of what she says to get by without paying any attention to it. At any point, if you asked me what she just said, I'd know. If you asked me what she said before that, I wouldn't have any idea. And if she asks a question, I'll catch that. Occasionally I might nod, or say, "Uh-huh," or something like that, just to show I'm following her, but that's about it.

It's like listening to the dispatcher on the cab radio. I have to pay some attention. If he calls my cab number, I have to catch that. And I need to hear some of the other things that come up, like open calls at hotels, announcements, emergencies, anything like that. But most of the traffic on the radio is just an endless run of cab numbers and addresses that have nothing to do with me, and I don't have to follow them too closely. So I don't. I let it all go by until I hear something—like my cab number— that tells me to listen. The difference is, the dispatcher isn't right here, expecting a little human contact.

Wait a second. What about right action? Compassion for all beings? Loving-kindness? Isn't listening part of right speech? Shouldn't I be looking for a way to help this woman with her troubles? Isn't that part of my practice?

On the other hand, she isn't really giving me much chance to take part in the conversation. She's just going on about her life. In fact, there is no conversation, just an endless drone from the back seat. She's not thinking about me, about my life, about what we might actually have in common. She's just thinking about herself, if she's thinking about anything at all.

She's not listening to me.

". . . and it's really a nice place to live, although it's funny, we still haven't gotten to know our neighbors, well, except for the Brombacks, they're really nice, but we don't really spend a lot of time with them or anything, we just get together . . ."

Face it. How often do you really listen to anyone? While they're talking, you're thinking about what you'll say next. You're wondering what they think of you. You're sizing them up, forming an opinion. Or you're wondering how you can wrap this up and move on. You're not really listening. It's not always like this, of course, but an awful lot of conversations really go nowhere at all. Because no one's listening.

Introductions are a great example:

"Hi, my name is Chris."

"Nice to meet you. I'm Brian."

Right away I think: what the hell did she say her name was?

It happens to everyone. You're thinking about how you look, what you're going to say, what you can do to make a good impression. Remembering her name would be a good start, but it doesn't happen. You weren't listening. (Here's a tip. When you meet someone, be sure to say their name: "Nice to meet you, Chris. I'm Brian." It's a big help. The trick is remembering to do it.)

Listening isn't that hard. It just takes a certain amount of respect for others. Empathy. Compassion. It also takes mindfulness, and we're trying to develop that. And it's worth the effort. When you listen to other people, you recognize their humanity, their uniqueness. Doing that, you get to move beyond your own self-involvement for a little while and open yourself to another point of view. So you might actually learn something.

Or you could gaze off at the urban sprawl and mumble, "Uh-huh," every thirty seconds or so.

". . . and with four kids, she's got her hands full, she doesn't have much time to work on her painting, which is too bad because she was really good at it, we all thought she'd go somewhere, but of course the kids are just angels, oh, it's the next right, just past that awful blue house there with the lawn that needs cutting, I don't know why they don't keep it neater, there's a neighborhood association . . ."

And of course, sometimes if you're not paying attention, you miss something you need to know. It might be hidden in there, and if you're just hearing what's being said without listening, you might miss it. But I catch that one. I make the right and coast down her street as she points out some of the houses, tells me a little about the people who live there.

Driving a cab—or doing anything that involves public contact—we have a chance to spread some good feeling in the world. We want to use our working day to make the world a better place, a little at a time. We're always planting seeds. That's part of practicing right livelihood. We want to leave the people we meet—and ourselves—a little better for the experience.

I pull in her driveway, and we settle up. Then, as she's opening the door, I smile and say, "I hope you have a good time with your daughter this weekend. You must be very proud of her."

She stops, looks at me, and smiles for the first time. "Thank you," she says. "That's very nice of you to say." She gets out, still smiling, happy because someone actually listened to her. Maybe she feels ignored, and it's hard on her, so she just tries harder to get some attention. But then, don't we all feel that way some of the time?

ON THE ROAD TO ROAD RAGE

I'm driving South Congress trying to get back to 6th Street to work the bar closings. It's one in the morning, and I don't even have my lease payment covered, so I'm a little on edge. I'm watching the traffic, gauging the lights ahead. If I work it right, I can load four or five more fares, make up for everything that went wrong on this shift.

A Silverado comes up on my left, moving fast, and then cuts in front of me and slows down suddenly. I hit the brakes, hear the tires squeal, feel the cab start to fishtail a little as the rear wheels threaten to break free. Just when I've got it under control, the Silverado slows again, makes a fast no-signal right turn onto East Annie and disappears. I'm gripping the wheel so hard, I think it's going to bend in my hands. For a moment I'm thinking I'll make the next turn, go after the son of a Beavis and give him a quick lesson in driving etiquette. Show him where the turn signal lever is.

I take a deep breath and let it out slowly. The moment passes.

You hear a lot about road rage these days. You see it a lot. Somehow it's been elevated to the status of a psychological condition, as if the people who give in to it are victims. Most road rage incidents are on the order of gestures, horn blasts, and bad language, drivers chasing each other around just to make some noise. But those encounters can escalate to something more serious. We all know better, but it's one thing to know better and another to let it go when it happens. Someone does something stupid, someone else responds, and before long, there's real trouble. Sometimes it ends with drivers going at it with tire irons. Sometimes there's a shooting, and it makes the evening news. It's happened in Austin, which isn't exactly the crime capital of America. And it's happened everywhere else.

You'd think road rage would have started when the first Model A was cut off by a horse-drawn buggy, but you'd be wrong. Road rage was unknown until the early 1980s, when a surge in violence on the roads was first reported in the media. Since then, it's been getting steadily worse.

By the way, all you Miami drivers, congratulations! A recently released survey shows that your city leads the nation in road rage incidents again this year. Way to go, Miamians. And stay out of Texas.

When a cabdriver thinks he's in trouble, he'll call for help and the company will send out a code 12 with his location over the radio. Drivers in the area respond. Many of these incidents involve some kind of road rage. Maybe the cabdriver cut someone off, or maybe he reacted to something the other driver did, but it winds up with them jawing in a parking lot, the cabdriver hoping some help will show up soon. If no punches are thrown in the first few minutes, help arrives and everyone calms down and goes back to what they were doing. Later, they have trouble remembering why they were so upset.

Of course, in those first few minutes, anything can happen.

There's only one sane way to react to the aggravations of the road: don't react. When someone cuts you off, just slow down, take it easy. Let them pull away. Then they won't be your problem. If you make a mistake and another driver starts yelling, carrying on, just give a little wave, act contrite. Don't respond, no matter what kind of mouth the other guy has. Whatever happens out there, just stay calm and let it go. In most cases, that will be the end of it. If it's not, head for a police station. Or a well-lit street with plenty of people around.

It's easy to say that. Let it go. Out on the street when you've just watched another driver swerve across three lanes of traffic with no warning, nearly wrecking your cab, it's another story. Your heart is hammering in your chest, adrenaline slamming you into a red rage. Maybe there's a passenger screaming, other drivers leaning on their horns. You have an urge to go after him, sit on his back bumper, let him know what you think. Maybe you can pull up even with him, roll down a window, and talk to him a little. "Hey Brainstorm, where'd you get that license? Kmart? Take it back, get your ten cents back." Something clever like that. Maybe he'll learn something, turn into a better driver. Out on the road at two in the morning, it can seem like a good idea. It's not.

Anger is just an emotion. It will pass. Usually a few minutes go by, then you think about it, realize it was just a mistake, a bad driver being even more stupid than usual. You realize it was just a bad moment. They happen. By then, you can be standing in a parking lot with a tire iron, saying some things you can't take back.

This is really about mindfulness. It's about getting hold of your anger before it pulls you into real trouble. That takes discipline, self-control. Mindfulness.

Anger is only an emotional state. It's impermanent. Empty. It's like fear or sadness or dejection. Or happiness, for that matter. It won't last. At its core, it's no more than a series of physical reactions that have a practical value in some situations but aren't much help out on the streets. Or anywhere else in the lives we live today. So we have to keep them from tearing us apart. And the key to that is to be aware of them as they come up.

Vietnamese Zen teacher Thich Nhat Hanh compares anger to a screaming baby. Mindfulness is the baby's attentive mother. The mother takes care of the baby, and soon the baby calms down. The mother doesn't make things worse with her own anger. And she doesn't turn away either. By paying attention to anger, we take away its power, and it just fades away on its own. In another analogy, anger is seen as a raging fire. Underlying thoughts and feelings feed it. By being mindful, we can recognize those thoughts and feelings for what they are without allowing them to feed the anger. Without fuel, the fire dies.

It's best not to fight against anger. Embrace it. Experience it. It's just another aspect of our everyday mind, the mind we want to understand. So anger provides us with an opportunity for growth. Feel it build. Let it go. Watch it as it ebbs away.

Anger often says something about who we are, what our state of mind is. An incident will drive us into a blind fury one day, but on another day the same incident won't affect us at all. Something trivial will set us off, while something truly serious won't. Seen this way, the idiots in traffic will just be idiots, good for a laugh, an occasional rush of adrenaline. They're not worth a spike in blood pressure. Or a street fight. Some good questions to ask are: Why am I angry about this? Why now?

But when you're out there on the street and you can feel it building inside you, it's hard to see it as an opportunity for growth. You want to give in. To act out. Just for a while. It's a little late for a nice round of zazen to calm the mind. Or an extensive behavior modification course in anger management. Here's an idea. Try chanting this short mantra three times: *Om ero-ba na-ra hum.* It's Tibetan. Roughly translated, it means, "The anger is in the air (or dispersed around you)." You can say it under your breath if you have passengers. Then take a deep, cleansing breath, exhale slowly, and let the anger out with it. This won't make the anger go away completely, but it will keep it from taking you over and getting you into trouble. Then you can embrace it and learn from it. *Om ero-ba na-ra hum.*

I know the streets are filled with really bad drivers who are always one weak moment away from disaster. At this hour, I know a lot of them are a little drunk. I expect the worst. When I'm right, why should I be upset? Maybe it's because I'm out here trying to make a living in a pretty hard world, and tonight it's not going that well. I'm struggling to make my expenses for the day, and I'm hurrying, not being as careful as I should be. If I'd worked harder earlier on, I wouldn't be in this position. Maybe I'm upset because I'm not happy about some of the other things going on in my life. I'm getting to know myself a little better, and I'm not satisfied with some of what I'm finding out. That could be a factor.

Now I'm crossing the bridge into downtown Austin. The Silverado is far away, the driver maybe already falling into bed to sleep it off. And I think how happy I am to be here, with the city lights ahead, people up on 6th Street just waiting for me to arrive so they can get in the cab and go home. And I'm happy I'm not in some parking lot with a drunk, waving a tire iron, talking a tough game, hoping I can get through this night alive.

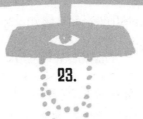

23.

LET'S FUCK WITH THE CABDRIVER

I pick them up outside Louie's downtown around nine, two young guys in sports coats, ties. They climb in the back, bumping around, settling in, laughing about something. I ask them where they're going, and they make me wait for it. I don't mind. I hit the meter and watch the traffic flowing past. I can sit here all night as long as the meter's going.

They're drunk.

Finally one of them tells me to take them to Sugar's, an upscale strip club a few miles north. I pull out, turn on Congress, then on 7th. They're talking quietly in the back and I tune them out, focus on driving. There's still a trace of light in the sky from the setting sun, the streets quiet.

"Hey, pal," one of them says. "What route you taking?"

"I'm going over to the interstate, then up to Koenig Lane, Highland Mall."

"Okay, bud. Just keeping an eye on you, that's all. I know how you cabdrivers like to run up the meter."

"Leave the man alone," the other says. "He knows what he's doing. He's a fucking expert. A real talented piece of shit."

"You shouldn't talk about him that way. He might be some psycho, looking for someone to go off on. You should apologize before he goes into a snit. Or starts crying."

"Sure. Hey, we're just kidding with you. No hard feelings, right buddy?"

"No problem."

"We don't want to get into it with you. You know, have a problem, anything like that." They're both laughing. "We wouldn't want that."

Uh-oh.

Most of the people who get in the cab are just regular people. Some are friendly, want to talk a little, some want to be left alone. Mostly, they want to get somewhere without a lot of drama. But once in a while, someone gets in who wants to play the classic game Let's Fuck with the Cabdriver. Usually they're young guys. Usually there are two of them, maybe three, trying to impress each other. Usually they're drunk.

I'm driving a little faster now. It's best to get these rides over with as quickly as possible, before things get worse. I take the ramp onto the interstate, pull out a few lanes, get it up to near sixty. Now they're getting on me about how rich they are, how they make in a day or two about what I make in a year. Sixty-five.

I'm taking a long bamboo breath, letting it out slowly, feeling the air on my lips. Then another. I'm practicing nonattachment. I'm practicing the paramita of patience. I'm spreading rays of good feelings through the cab. Loving-kindness. Compassion.

Who am I kidding? I'm only a beginner, not a buddha. I hate these guys. The Dalai Lama would want to wring their necks.

Some time ago, an Austin cabdriver killed two passengers with a gun he kept in the cab for protection. They'd been at a sports bar watching a Mike Tyson fight, and they'd been drinking. Maybe they were playing Let's Fuck with the Cabdriver. No one really knows what happened in the cab. The driver was the only one left to tell what happened. There was an argument. Some words were said. According to the driver, he had pictures of his family mounted on the dashboard, and the passengers made some comments about them. That set him off. The driver pulled over on a dark stretch of Barton Springs Road, and everyone got out. The driver pulled out a gun from under the seat and shot both men dead. The second man was running away when he was shot in the back. The driver died a few months later in a jail cell while awaiting trial. He became severely depressed, lost fifty pounds, and died of heart failure.

I never met the man. By all accounts, he'd been coming unglued for a while. His life hadn't been going well, and he wasn't handling it. He wasn't someone who should have been carrying a gun in a cab. I don't know anyone who should.

That wouldn't happen to me. I meditate. I have compassion for all beings. And I don't carry a gun.

A ride like this is good practice. I have to take the long view, have some perspective. Everything they're saying should just roll away from me. I'm not rich. I don't have status or power. That's all right. It's nothing I didn't know. Those things don't really matter. Wealth and power are distractions that keep us from seeing the world as it is. They keep us from seeing our own true nature. I'm better off without them. What matters is this road I'm driving. The path. The Eightfold Freeway. Dharma Road.

The Buddha had to deal with some hard people, and he did it with style. He lived in a time of lawlessness and relative anarchy. At one time, there was a fearsome bandit named Angulimala who roamed the country-side killing and robbing whoever he came across. The Buddha sought him out and faced him with compassion and great courage. This courage from an unarmed monk impressed the bandit and made him think about his own actions. The Buddha helped Angulimala free himself from the conditions that had led him down the path of lawlessness and converted him to the dharma. Angulimala became a monk and dedicated the rest of his life to living in peace.

The courage and compassion of the Buddha are legendary. In his old age, he was challenged by an upstart monk named Devadatta, who wanted to take over the movement. When Devadatta conspired to have the Buddha killed, soldiers were sent out, but the Buddha instructed them in the dharma and they went away, changed forever. Devadatta even sent a vicious elephant to trample the Buddha, but the Buddha petted him and taught him about karma and the unfolding of his future lives. The elephant backed away, also changed. Devadatta was finally defeated. The Buddha did all this by being calm and showing great compassion. The charisma helped.

I'd like to be able to do all that and more. I'd like to save these toxic passengers from themselves. I'd like to lead them into the dharma and send them down the path with a kind word and an easy smile. I'm not ready. I can't help them. All I can do is not react to them. Maybe someday I'll be able to do more.

I'm getting off the interstate now. Only a few more minutes. I can take a few more minutes. This is only another trial, another opportunity for growth. The light ahead goes red. Okay. It'll be a little longer. I can handle this.

They're still talking. I don't even want to repeat what they're saying now. I start to smile. This isn't so bad. It's only talk. I don't' have to get pulled in to their games. I can even have a little fun with them. I pull up at the light, turn halfway around, and look at them. I give them a little smile. A friendly, helpful look. Like the Buddha would do. They shut up, look at me. "Can I ask you a question?"

"Heh, heh. Yeah sure, asswipe. Go ahead. Ask away."

"Have you accepted Jesus Christ as your personal savior?"

Suddenly it's quiet in the cab. They mumble something, and then their voices trail off. The light changes, and I start up. As drunk as they are, they're not going to play Let's Fuck with Our Lord and Savior. It works every time.

I make it the rest of the way in silence. When I pull up at Sugar's, they drop a twenty over the seat and get out without saying a word. As I'm pulling away, I can see one of the Sugar's door guys talking to them, checking them out. He's about six-five, two-fifty, and he's not going to listen to any of their nonsense. And he's not going to let them in the club either. They must have said something he didn't like. As I pull out onto the street, I watch them waving at me in my rear-view mirror. They need a cab. I drive down the road, already forgetting about them.

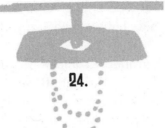

NOT MUCH TO FEAR

Three in the morning, I'm making a last pass down 6th Street, trying to load one last fare for the night. There are some small groups of people around, stragglers, mostly people who work at the clubs, some die-hards who don't really want to go home.

A woman in a light blue blouse and chinos steps out from a group in front of the Blind Pig and waves at me. She looks a little high. At this hour, a lot of people are. I stop, and she gets in with two men, gives me the address of an apartment complex off Riverside Drive. I make a couple turns, head east to the interstate, then south. They're talking quietly in the back, and I'm picking up on a couple words here and there. They're talking about scoring some rock. Crack cocaine. Well, it's three in the morning—things like this happen. I wish they'd happen to someone else. Really, I wish they wouldn't happen at all.

I could give them a nice speech about the dangers of crack, about the trail of devastation it leaves in its wake.

I've seen a little of that. Enough to know. (Although I've never been stupid enough to try it myself.) I could talk to them about the Fifth Grave Precept, the one that bans the use of intoxicants. I could warn them that crack won't help them to see through the veil of delusion and discover their own true nature. Or to help all beings. For that matter, I could tell them it might kill them. Fast and ugly.

I keep driving. I'm guessing they know all they want to know about that. And they don't care.

We get there and I turn, smile at them. "Nine dollars," I say.

"Oh, we're just stopping here for a few minutes. Then we're going down to Stassney Lane. Is that all right?"

"Sure. Someone has to stay in the cab, though."

That's no problem. One guy gets out the passenger side and the others stay in the cab. They're nervous, a little jumpy, like they're not sure they're going to score. They're hoping. We all sit there in silence, waiting to see.

The guy comes back after a couple minutes. He gets in, looking glum. "He's out," he mumbles under his breath. "We'll have to go see Tonio."

There's mumbling in the back seat. They aren't happy about this. I don't think they like Tonio. Finally, one of them gives me an address in East Austin, a downscale neighborhood, one I like to avoid, asks if that's all right.

The meter's up to $10.50. Up to there and then down to Stassney. Sure, no problem. This is, after all, a business.

Okay. Let's stop for a moment, take stock. It's after three in the morning and I'm riding around with a cab full of crackheads out trying to score. You're reading this, wondering, what in the name of the Sixth Patriarch is this guy thinking? He's going to get himself shot. You see this happen in those eighties movies, the ones with the Hill Street vibe, the gritty urban realism. The one where the cabdriver always gets shot. For some people, this would be their worst nightmare played out in real life.

I'm not worried. For one thing, they're being polite, trying to stay on my good side. They don't seem dangerous. They're really kind of pathetic, just victims of their own weakness, sucked down into something they can't control. Plus, like most addicts, they're not in the best shape. If it comes to it, I could probably pull out the pepper spray, throw a few punches, handle it that way. Then call the police. I think I can handle this.

Unless they have guns. In Texas, that's always a possibility. But they're wearing light clothes, the guys in T-shirts, and it doesn't look like they're armed.

So I'm not that worried. It's an adventure, something to make my night a little more interesting.

This might be a good time to mention compassion. We're supposed to have compassion for all beings—including crackheads. Active empathy. Crack is a hard road down, and the bottom is a bad place to be. It's lead-pipe certain their lives are going to get worse before they get better. It's likely that one of these riders will be dead in a year or two. Maybe they'll all be. And what's worse, there's a sadness about these people that says they're well aware of what's happening to them, and they're helpless to stop it. There's not much I can do about any of this, but I can treat them with a little respect. Maybe that will help.

I head for the address on the east side, get there with the meter up to $19.50. It's the same drill—the one guy gets out, goes up to a little shotgun shack with a rusting Oldsmobile up on blocks, lawn furniture set up by the front door. It's quiet out here, pretty dark. I'm wondering if APD is watching the place. It happens. I'm wondering what I'd say if I got pulled over on the way out. It occurs to me how strange it is that I'm more worried about the police than a car full of crackheads. A few minutes later, he comes out, trying to act tough and cool, but smiling. He scored. I can hear sighs of relief in the back seat. I'm a little relieved myself.

Fifteen minutes later, I pull into the lot of an apartment complex on Stassney. They get out, still being polite, but pretty anxious to get inside. I pocket thirty-seven dollars (with a three dollar tip) and head for home.

Driving a cab at night, you get used to being in some strange situations. It doesn't bother you as much, and you get a sense about the people. My first few months, I got scared any number of times, but nothing happened. I didn't know what to expect. Then I got used to it, more comfortable. Now, I don't worry too much about what might happen.

That doesn't mean I'm careless. I'm not. Cabdriving is one of the world's most dangerous occuptions. A cabdriver is more likely to die on the job that a police officer—or most other workers. I'll take a good look at people before they get in the cab. If someone looks like real trouble, I'll just keep going. And given a choice, I'll skip the drug runs, although there's usually not much of a choice. By the time I figure out what's going on, it's a little late to do anything about it except play along and keep my eyes open.

A while ago, I had to contact the IRS. I wasn't in any trouble. In fact, I had some money coming due to a really stupid mistake I'd made on my return. I was terrified. I could picture some IRS agent calling up every piece of information about me on the government's megaflop computer system, going over it, looking for some way to turn it around, soak me for whatever I'd managed to put in the bank. And then toss me in jail, just for laughs. It was all I could do to punch the toll-free number into the phone.

The representative was very nice, very helpful. When we were done, he told me to have a nice day, and he sounded like he meant it. And before long, I got a full refund of what I'd overpaid.

Fear is a useful emotion. Without it, our ancestors would have been slaughtered by lions on the savanna and we wouldn't be here to talk about it. Fear triggers the fight-or-flight reflex, which promotes a range of physical reactions that help us to escape danger.

The problem is that we don't live in the wild, and in the world we do live in, fear only weakens us. The fight-or-flight reaction just doesn't work here. And many of the fear-provoking situations we face last for a long time, leading to physical and emotional problems that are more serious than the problems that triggered the fear in the first place.

We fear the unknown. We don't fear the known. We fear the future. We don't fear the present. Right now I'm driving down the interstate in light traffic, doing my job. Right now I'm having some coffee, dialing the number for the IRS. Right now, everything is pretty much all right. If we live in the present, we've really got nothing to fear. But we don't do that. Our minds are always making up stories about the misery (or the utter bliss) that lies just ahead. They're just stories. And they're almost always wrong. Things go wrong all the time, but they're rarely the things we were worried about. We worry about a cab full of crackheads, but they get out of the cab and we get blindsided by a bus instead. Maybe because we were so worried about the crackheads, we forgot to look out for the bus.

After the 9/11 attacks, there was an outbreak of fear in the United States and around the world. The mood changed in one morning. People began watching the skies for low-flying planes and checking the mail for white powder. And what happened? The world continued to warm. Oil supplies dwindled. Wars in Iraq and Afghanistan drained the national spirit. A tsunami swamped the coast of Asia. New Orleans was flooded and nearly destroyed. The world economy melted down. There were a few minor incidents of terrorism, but nothing on the scale of the fear that gripped the world immediately after the attacks.

That's why they call it terrorism.

There's a difference between fear and caution. Of course, we should take steps to prevent further attacks. We should also deal with global warming, the financial crisis, and the many other problems we face. But we shouldn't act from fear. It just clouds our judgment and makes it harder to deal with the world as it is.

By the way, in case you haven't heard, according to the Mayan calendar the world will end on December

21, 2012. Worried? Don't be. If it happens, it happens. There's nothing we can do.

Right now, the world has not ended. So let's deal with that.

We can learn something about ourselves from looking at our fears. I'm afraid of heights, but I've stood at the edge of thousand-foot cliffs and looked down with no problem. I worry about bad news in the mail or over the phone, but I never seem to get any. I fear the IRS and the police. I'm pretty worried about the government in general. I fear situations I can't control. Crackheads don't worry me all that much.

I heard a dharma talk once in which a Zen teacher described her job as simply helping her students to master their fears.

Compassion and mindfulness practice can help put things in perspective. We can take our fears out and have a good look at them. We find they are only temporary states of mind. They're impermanent, like everything else. Just states of mind that will pass if we let them. We've been afraid of one thing or another for much of our lives, but those fears have generally faded away. Recognizing this can help us deal with our anxiety over the future.

But when you're out on a dark street and Freddy Krueger gets in the cab and tells you to take him to the Bates Motel, it's hard to just let go of fear. The problem is that our thoughts and feelings run in cycles. Fear leads to more fear. We get hung up. We feel the fear, and we think about what we're afraid of, and this just leads to more fear. When this happens, we have to stop the destructive cycle we're in and take a new, more constructive direction. A mantra might help, like the one for road rage. Here's another mantra: *Is this helpful?* Meaning, is the paralyzing fear you're feeling helping you to deal with a difficult and possibly dangerous situation? Or is it only making things worse? Say this to yourself a few times. Hopefully it will break the cycle you're stuck in. And then you can do something useful to deal with the situation.

Like find a well-lit area with people around where you can tell Freddy to get the hell out of the cab.

There's a Buddhist practice in which we come face-to-face with our deepest fears. If you're afraid of snakes, get a bag of snakes and just face them down. Doing this, you can overcome your fear of snakes and your fear of fear itself. Psychologists use a similar practice to help patients gradually overcome the phobias that cripple them. Like the fear of flying. Doing that, we can see that the reality seldom lives up to the images we create for ourselves. It's really the unknown that scares us. The devil we don't know. Once we've faced our fears, they won't trouble us again.

The same is true of other destructive feelings, like guilt and resentment. And hatred. When we confront them squarely, we find that the problems they cause in our personal and spiritual lives are more harmful for us than the situations that caused them in the first place. And when we see that, we can let them go. It's all part of a journey of self-discovery.

And that's the journey we're on.

THE SANGHA GANG

I pull into line at the airport, and I look around at the drivers in the lot. It's an impressive sight. There are usually sixty or eighty drivers there, sometimes more, all of them killing time while they wait for their next fare. There are games of chess going on at the tables, poker games with stones for chips. There are drivers with lawn chairs reading in the grass, small groups standing around talking. Then a few of them get in their cabs and pull up to the terminal to load, and some others pull into the lot. This goes on all day and well into the night.

The drivers come from all over. There are Nigerians, Russians, a few Frenchmen, a lot of drivers who don't seem to be from anywhere you could name, but they're not from around here. The American drivers come from around the country. There are Anglos, Blacks, Latinos, Creoles. Rednecks with NASCAR bumper stickers. Brothers in dashikis.

Out here on Dharma Road, we're all just cabdrivers.

When the dispatcher puts out a Code 12 for cabs in

the area to help a driver in trouble, everyone goes. No one calls in to ask who it is. The drivers just help each other. It's a given, one of the rules of the road. There's a feeling that we're all in this together, we've got to help each other out, because no one else will.

Not that the drivers all like each other. They don't. It's like any other group of people. There are arguments, even an occasional fistfight. Supposedly, there was a knife fight over a big fare in front of the airport terminal, but that was a very long time ago. If it really happened. It might be just a story someone made up on a slow night at the airport. Another urban cabdriving legend.

Out on the streets, the drivers look out for each other. You'll see a couple drivers getting into it, and then a few hours later, one of them is giving the other a jump start. I've gone on rescue missions, helping a driver in trouble, wound up in a tense situation in a parking lot. And this for someone I barely know. While it's happening, we're buddies. Then it's over and we move on, maybe never say another word to each other.

In Buddhism, a spiritual community is called a sangha. It's one of the Three Treasures: Buddha, Dharma, and Sangha (the example set by the Buddha, the teachings he left us, and the community we practice with).

I don't have a sangha.

That's the problem with a modern real-life Zen practice like mine. I'm pretty much out on my own, figuring it out as I go. It's partly my own fault. I keep to myself, and I don't go looking for people to share my practice with. There must be some around, but I don't know where. And I don't have a lot of time to go looking. That's all right, it's just the way it is. I've had teachers, but I don't have one now. I might be able to send an email to a Facebook group when I have a problem with my practice, but I'm not really a Facebook kind of guy. It's not the same as sitting down for *dokusan* (a one-on-one interview) with a real Zen master. And I don't have a group of dharma friends to spend time with. People I can talk to about my practice. People I can ask for advice.

I've been involved with sanghas in the past, just on a temporary basis, and it's a big help. When I'm in the cab out at the airport or sitting at a cabstand talking with the other drivers, we usually talk about cabdriving. There are always rumors floating around, stories, maybe half of them true. It's mostly a way of killing time, but it's also a good way of learning about cabdriving. It's the same with a sangha. In a sangha, most of the people don't really know each other outside of the zendo. So the main topic of conversation is practice, and it's a good way of learning. Just knowing that other people are struggling with the same problems you're struggling with—and that some of them are making progress—is a great help.

Besides, from what I've seen, they're pretty nice people.

Before the Buddha's enlightenment, he practiced with a small group of five ascetics, part of a larger community of seekers in an area known as the Deer Park. They parted ways when he gave up the ascetic life. When he became enlightened and decided to teach, he returned to his five friends and gave his first sermon—the one about suffering and the end of suffering. They were his first disciples, and they stayed with him until he died. Before long, they were joined by other seekers, and after that, the Buddha was always the center of a large spiritual community. A sangha.

The sangha is not an absolute requirement for practice. There are no absolute requirements. There is a tradition of lone monks living in caves in the mountains of Tibet.

The *lung gompas* are another Tibetan tradition. They walk in solitude on the high trails of the Himalayas, breathing the thin air and chanting, oblivious to the cold. There was also a long history of forest monks in Southeast Asia. Through the centuries, they roamed the forests of the area, living off the land and practicing diligently.

If you're living in Wyoming, in Kenya, or at a research station in the Antarctic, you probably don't have a sangha either. They're usually found in major cities, and even there, some people just aren't joiners. Not everyone fits in easily with a group. I don't. That's all right. It makes practice harder, but it's no reason to give up. It's just another hurdle to overcome. I like to picture myself as a forest monk, living in a modern forest of glass and steel and too much asphalt, being as diligent about my practice as I can be. And I don't have to worry about being eaten by tigers.

There's another reason to have hope for my practice—something that can give us all reason to hope. When he sat down under the bodhi tree, the Buddha didn't have a sangha either. He was on his own, discouraged and destitute, without even a plan. He had failed at everything he'd tried. He only had a tree to sit under and the morning star. And he had his determination. For him, that was enough.

Maybe it can be enough for me.

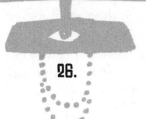

IN THE SHALLOW END

Tuesday morning I have a few minutes, so I turn on the TV, just to see what's going on in the world. I flip through the channels. Not much. Tyra has a theme show about beauty emergencies. On the late edition of *Today*, a celebrity chef is whipping up veal something in nice beds of arugula. The ladies of *The View* are having a very sympathetic discussion of Lindsay Lohan's latest brush with lunacy. I hit the remote once more and *The Price is Right* leaps out. That about does it for me.

Apparently, nobody blew anything up overnight, which is what I really wanted to find out. The world limps into another day. Good enough. Time to go.

Out on the road, I have to listen to the passengers talk about the way their lives are going. It's not fun, but it's part of the job. My first trip, I take two businessmen to the airport. They spend the time complaining about the hotel van being out of service, forcing them to take a cab. The horror! They don't think they'll stay at that hotel again.

Later, I load two women at Barton Creek Square mall going back to the Sheraton. They have bags. Lots of bags. Apparently, it's pretty much all clothes. And shoes. All the way downtown, they talk about the things they bought and the things they saw that they didn't buy. They're pretty excited. The way it sounds, they'll be going back to the mall very soon.

Don't get me wrong. I'm not immune. Today I'm wearing my new Hawaiian shirt. (Well, it's not new—I got it at a Goodwill store, the only place to buy really good Hawaiian shirts.) I'm pretty excited about it. It's a deep purple with red and orange dancing girls on beaches of yellow sand. And pineapples. Lots of pineapples. I've got about a dozen shirts more-or-less like it in the closet, and I was excited about all of them when I first got them. The excitement fades faster than the colors.

I do the Sudoku puzzle in the local paper. (Du yu Sudoku? I du.) I follow sports, the local teams. I read crime novels in the airport line. I tape TV shows to watch when I get off work, go to a movie once in a while.

These things are only distractions. There's nothing wrong with them, but they won't help me move down that Eightfold Freeway. They won't help me move down any path at all. They just keep me occupied. It's the same with shopping. It's only a distraction from the things in life that really matter. I should do more zazen and volunteer at an orphanage, but I just checked out season three of *Battlestar Galactica* from the library, so I'll be watching that tonight.

Still later in the afternoon, I take a cabaret dancer home from a hair salon. She makes me roll up all the windows to preserve the perfect shape of her new 'do.

When she gets out, she holds her head unnaturally still as she walks away.

After that, I pick up a poodle from a dog-grooming salon. She's going home with her new 'do. That's right, my fare is a poodle. What does this say about the way my life is going? She sits in the back seat and pants at the window. She doesn't say much, but she does look nice.

In the evening, I load a couple of fares from the trendy restaurants downtown. There's a lot of lively discussion about the meal, most of it critical. This was a little salty, that was slightly undercooked. The presentation was ordinary. Presentation. They just spent more than I make in a day on a designer meal, and they didn't even enjoy it. One couple has an actual argument in the cab over the merits of various styles of Japanese cuisine. Tempers are raised. I'm guessing they hit the sake bar pretty hard after dinner. When they get out, they're not speaking.

It's getting crowded in the shallow end of the pool.

I get a little cynical listening to the people out here. All the cabdrivers get this way after awhile. I don't want to, but I can't help it. I know this says as much about me as it does about the world I live in, but there it is.

This is the way the world is.

We live in a world with sneakers that light up as we run. Robotic pets. Plastic surgery for non-robotic dogs. We have fitness water, which turns out to be tap water in a pretty bottle for a couple bucks. We have cars that talk to us, but they don't have much to say.

We live in a world where 2.7 billion people live on less than two dollars a day. There's a war on, and it's not going that well for anybody. Natural resources are running out, the planet is heating up, and the environment is deteriorating. People don't want to think about any of that, so they immerse themselves in the most trivial activities they can find. And then they're so busy analyzing them that they don't even enjoy them.

Or, to be fair, they go to a Goodwill store and buy a gently used Hawaiian shirt.

Buddhist practice helps us to see through the delusions of everyday life and take a wider view of the world. We do that by looking deep within ourselves and seeing our true nature. But the culture of the twenty-first century is not oriented toward self-discovery or self-realization. Sogyal Rinpoche describes modern society as "a celebration of all the things that lead away from the truth, make truth hard to live for and discourage people from even believing that it exists." We are constantly seduced by the promises of our consumer society and the hope that we can find happiness simply by gratifying our senses.

Cabdrivers listen to a lot of people talking about their lives, about what's important to them. We don't usually want to hear about it, but we're stuck in the car, so we can't help it. And people aren't careful about what they say in cabs. We'll never see each other again anyway. Most of the conversations I hear have something to do with making more money and using it to buy more happiness. And the people talking don't sound especially happy. I almost never hear people talk about the state of the world or about any kind of spirituality, or about anything else that seems like it really matters. And I don't hear them talk about how full and happy their lives are either.

That's the human condition, twenty-first-century style. That's what passes for our true nature in this world we've made. We're never satisfied. We always want more, and more never seems to help.

(By the way, are you tired of paying too much for car insurance? Click here and tell us a little about yourself. Remember, the more you buy, the more you save. Because you're worth it!)

Buying a way out of the human condition might seem like a good idea. But it doesn't work. Remember, we talked about Elvis, about how he suffered? If that approach worked at all, it would have worked for him. It didn't. And it doesn't work for anyone else either.

In Tibetan Buddhism, people who are controlled by their cravings are reincarnated as a lesser form of life called a hungry ghost. These beings live in a hell of their own making. They eat all the time, but they are always hungry, never full. To me, that sounds like a metaphor for life in twenty-first-century America. And about half of the rest of the world.

All the distractions of our modern world are impermanent. Empty. It's all appearance. They only distract us from any real understanding of this world and our place in it. We crave, we grasp, we hold on as best we can, but none of it will last. And the satisfaction we feel is the most transient of all. In no time it is gone, replaced by new cravings. This is our life today. This is our fate, if we accept it.

Our personal problems are also impermanent. The emotional crises will pass, and the psychodramas will fade away. They will all be resolved in some way and replaced by new problems, and we'll struggle to deal with those. The crises come and go until we do something to change ourselves. They won't be resolved by any shopping spree. Sometimes I wish I could just give in to the distractions of the senses, sink into a life of self-indulgence. Sometimes I think I could learn to like French cuisine. Or develop a taste for fine clothing. It's not going to happen. It's not my nature. It's just not me.

Besides, I can't afford it. That's one of the benefits of cabdriving. It limits your options. You can't really sell out. There aren't any buyers.

It's a Tuesday night, and there's really not much going on, not much reason to stay out late. I head home around midnight, thinking I'm due for a break from the usual madness. I've got a bacon cheeseburger and curly fries from Jack in the Box. No presentation, but I'm hungry and I'll savor it. I've got that *Battlestar Galactica* DVD to watch while I eat. It's guaranteed to be full of plot holes and gimmicks, but I don't mind. I'll enjoy it all the same. I'll lounge around in old jeans and a paint-stained T, making the most of each moment, whatever it holds.

That's the key. Making the most of it, whatever it is. There are highs and lows in life. They all count. If you're climbing Mount Everest, be sure to enjoy the view. If you're cleaning the rooms in a seedy motel, find a way to make that worthwhile. Life can be a lot of fun, but you have to actually live it. If you're only filling your time with distractions to avoid something deeper, you're wasting it. You'd be better off behind the wheel of a cab, out here driving down Dharma Road. Making the most of that.

A DRIVE DOWN PARTY LANE

The middle of August is a great time for an Austin cab-driver. Prime time. The college kids come back early here, a few weeks before Labor Day. Classes don't get going right away, so they all head for 6th Street to get back into the action. The locals are out in force, letting off their own steam. And it's a hundred degrees every day, ninety at night. Which really reminds you: this is Texas, you might as well enjoy it.

Some of them enjoy it a little too much.

I'm working 6th Street tonight. It's a Wednesday, but it looks like a Saturday. There's a little drizzle in the air, but not enough to send anyone home. I'm checking the cab-stands, trolling the side streets, like always. A kid gets in the cab at Trinity—he's underage, looks about sixteen. He's had a few, then a few after that, getting the most out of his fake ID. I ask where he's going and don't get an answer, so I take a good look at him. He's going to be sick, and soon.

"There's a fifty-dollar clean-up fee if you puke in my cab," I tell him. "And I won't be cleaning it up. You will."

He tries to focus, gets an idea where he is. He looks confused, like he doesn't know what he's doing in a cab. He opens the door and gets out. He walks a few feet and trips on the cobblestones, goes down in a heap. From there he crawls to a trash can, pulls himself up, and throws up into it. Then he folds up and passes out right there on the sidewalk. Everyone looks around for a cop to come along and take him away. This close to the cabstand, it won't take long. A couple of drivers are already headed out to look for someone to get him in a wagon and out of there.

A couple gets in the cab and I pull away, headed for the Marriott. They're drunk, and they're having a fight, getting into it right in the back of the cab. The guy was checking out the waitress, so she made a scene; now they're in the back of a cab screaming at each other, dragging out all the baggage of an unhappy marriage. I'm thinking, *Can't they at least wait until they get back to the hotel to do this?*

I drop them off and get a radio call to meet APD in front of Beerland, a rock club on Red River. When I pull up, two cops are having a conversation with a kid in his twenties. He isn't holding up his end of the conversation. He's gazing off at the night with a vacant smile on his face. One of the cops signals me to stay in the cab. There's a sign out front listing the bands: Microwave World. Dirt Track Brawlers. Divorcers. Sounds like a fun night. Some serious musicians on the bill. There's a thick bass rattle from inside the club, bored-looking kids hanging out on the sidewalk, smoking cigarettes. Watching the cops.

Finally, one of the cops comes over, tells me to forget about it. "The guy's dusted," he says. "We can't even get an address out of him. We're gonna take him in, try to get him some help. Sorry for the trouble."

I tell him no problem and drive off. Driving nights, I see a lot of this. People go out to have a good time, and most of them do, but sometimes the good time just leads somewhere else. Somewhere pretty dark. Sometimes it's drugs, alcohol. Sometimes it's just the way things are. The human race, growing up. Or trying to.

Don't misunderstand. Most of the people out here are having a real good time. This is the high point of the week for them, the time when they can put aside the jobs and responsibilities that hang over their days and just let loose for a while. It's great to be out with your friends, hearing some of that fine Austin music, feeling real good. I can hear a crowd inside a piano bar singing "Rocket Man" real loud. They sound pretty happy. And that's great. Good for them.

But it can slide over the edge pretty easily.

Stopped at a light, I see a woman standing alone on the sidewalk wearing a T-shirt that says, *Drink till you want me.* It's a funny shirt, but she's not laughing. She doesn't look happy at all.

It's like the Tom Waits line: "The streets aren't for dreaming now."

I don't claim to be holier than thou. Or anyone else either. I've had a few problems on my own road. I used to say, "I'll try anything once." That's not a healthy attitude, in case you're wondering. Sometimes once can be one time too many. But it's how you learn. I'd go into more detail about that, but I'm not sure how the statute of limitations works. I don't want to self-incriminate. Or embarrass myself. But I usually just wanted to have a little fun, and a few times, it went off the tracks.

I'm back at 6th working the side streets. Tonight the streets look like a scene from *Blade Runner*, all wet asphalt and colored lights flashing, people in loose lines on the sidewalks. On Red River, there are kids out selling crack on the corners, a block from the police station. There are flyers up for a rave tomorrow night, and the letter *X* is all over them. Driving up 8th, I can see kids passing around joints in the parking lots, coked out jivers dancing down the sidewalks. There are pillheads and junkies out on the streets tonight. I'm out here too, just trying to get by. Trying to become enlightened and save all beings. But I've got no idea how to save anyone. Not in a world like this.

This chapter is not about drugs. I know, it seems like it is, but that's not really the point.

This chapter is about emptiness. And the ways we try to fill it.

In Afghanistan, the opium trade is booming since the invasion. Oddly enough, the people of Afghanistan have little interest in opium. Or in heroin. Or in any other drug. You'd think between the ongoing wars, the religious strife and the grinding poverty, they'd welcome the oblivion. If I had to live in a hellhole like Afghanistan, I'd be doing so much smack I'd embalm myself.

We live in the richest society in the world's history. We have choices beyond the dreams of anyone who lived before us and beyond the hopes of most of the world's six billion people. We should be coasting along, enjoying our lives in the world's richest society. And some people are. But this culture is proof that riches can't buy salvation. Or even peace of mind. Too many of us need something more to make our lives seem full and satisfying. When we get it, it still won't be enough. And we'll look for something else.

The problem isn't the drugs. Drugs are just a symptom of something deeper. Something much harder to deal with. Human nature. If there were no drugs, we'd still feel the emptiness, and we'd still look for ways to fill it. We talked about shopping and designer food, about trying to fill the emptiness with material things. Drugs are just another way of doing that. It's as if the people on the street tonight are going shopping for something to make it all fit together. The next high is like a new pair of shoes or a fine meal at Cafe Whosis. Or my new Hawaiian shirt. It's great for a while, but it doesn't last long.

This is the Four Noble Truths being played out before our eyes. We suffer because we crave what we don't have. We are slaves to our desires. And our desires have a life of their own. The more we indulge ourselves in them, the more our cravings grow. We keep reaching out for more, but we can never have enough. And in the end, this leads to trouble. The Buddha showed us that there is a way out of this. There is a way to control our desires and ease our suffering. That way is the Eightfold Path.

As we become more mindful of the effect of our cravings, we can put them in perspective and go about our lives without being caught up in those cravings. And in the end, we'll be better off.

Each of us can embrace the Eightfold Path and find a way out of this dilemma. But our culture of self-indulgence has consequences for people everywhere. Our consumer culture has led to environmental destruction, economic exploitation, brutal wars, and grinding poverty for many around the world. The Second Noble Truth—that we suffer due to attachment—is being played out on a global scale, and it's hard to see the world embracing the Eightfold Path anytime soon. What's needed is a more engaged Buddhism, acting constructively to make the world a better place for all. But that has to begin with personal commitment. We can start by living our own lives mindfully, having a positive effect on the world in our own small way. And hoping others will do the same.

There's not much I can do about world hunger. I can't stop the wars. I'm out here in a cab, and all I can do is to get people where they're going and try to brighten their days just a little, help them keep a positive attitude. That's Right Livelihood. It's a good place to start. It's a step.

I'm committed to taking this path. But I'm only a beginner. A rookie. Deep down, there's a part of me that just wants to fire up a fat one, or get lost with a mirror and a straw. Or suck down some Jack Daniel's and go out onto the street tonight and just let go, let all those demons out, see what they want to do.

But I'm not going to do any of that. I'm past that, more or less. I've learned. Cravings are only cravings. They arise, and they fade away like smoke rings in the night air. Like clouds that cover the sun for a few seconds, then blow away. Like thoughts that come up during zazen. I just notice them, and then let them go. I don't attach to them. The fact that I'd still like to have a drink or a couple of lines is one more thing I know about myself. I don't even have to overcome my cravings. I just have to let them go. It's not as hard as it once seemed.

In fact, it's not hard at all.

By one in the morning, things are getting a little wild, even for 6th Street. Some of the college kids are out of practice, not handling the Jell-O shots that well. There are people dancing around, doing coyote howls. A few fights break out. The cops have a wagon parked on the corner and they're working on filling it up. Another fun night on Party Lane.

I load on San Jacinto and take a man to a small house in South Austin. He tells me he's a recovering alcoholic—he'd gone down to 6th Street just wanting to hear some music, but he couldn't handle it. All the drinking going on, it was all he could do to get out of there without having a few, getting back on that slow train to his own personal hell. As I pull up at his house, he asks me if I know where he can score some pot.

I pause for a second. "Sorry, man," I tell him. "I'm trying to stay away from that."

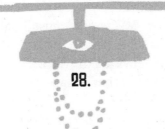

KARMA FOR KABBIES

The drivers sitting in line at the airport think they know something about karma. The fares at the terminal are assigned randomly. The driver at the front of the line gets the next passenger, so there's no hustling for fares, no way for the drivers to line up the long trips or duck the short ones. So it's all pure chance and, in the long run, the fares even out. Still, it always seems like some of the drivers are doing well, others are sinking badly. There are streaks and slumps. Waiting in line, the drivers talk about how the day is going, what kind of fares they've been getting. It goes something like this:

"Man, I can't believe it. I waited two hours and got a six-buck trip right over there off Riverside Drive. I haven't had a trip over twelve bucks all day. It's my karma coming back at me. I must have done something really bad in a past life to deserve this."

"Hey, guys, how you doin'? I just got back from Fort Hood, got a flat rate, hundred and twenty, plus a twenty-dollar tip. Before that I had a forty-dollar ride out to

Cedar Park. With these gorgeous models, you should have seen them. My karma must finally be coming around. Must be all those good deeds I've been thinking about doing. You guys makin' the big ones too?"

That's the popular view of karma. A cosmic system of rewards and punishments, meted out by some ultimate power far beyond our understanding. But that's not how it works. That's all just the luck of the draw. It'll even out—maybe not the part about the gorgeous models, but the rest of it will.

Karma is simply the law of cause and effect. The most obvious type of karma is the familiar, straightforward kind of cause and effect. Physics is karma. The sun revolves around the galactic center, the earth revolves around the sun, the moon revolves around the earth. If you throw a stone into the lake, it will make a splash and send out ripples. If you slam your cab into a telephone pole, the front end will be crushed, you'll suffer a concussion from the air bag, and you'll be unemployed before the wrecker shows up. Cause and effect.

Karma has been compared to planting seeds. If you plant an acorn, an oak tree will grow. If you plant a garden in the spring, you'll be eating fresh vegetables in the summer. If you plant seeds of hate, hate will be the result. If you plant seeds of loving-kindness, loving-kindness will grow within you.

On a personal level, karma is psychology. Our personalities are formed by karma. The Buddha said that our minds are the result of all our previous thoughts. Our thoughts and our moods are impermanent. They arise and they fall away. But they don't just vanish. Other thoughts and moods rise from them. Over time, our thoughts form a pattern, and this pattern guides our thoughts. We fall into habits. We think a certain way, and we don't think in other ways. The longer this goes on, the harder it is to break out of these patterns. And, being human, we're not very careful about what kind of habits we fall into. We take the easy way out, and the easy way gets easier. Before long, it's the only way.

Out on the streets, we're in a hurry, so we push the speed limit a little, and then a little more. We start hanging out with the other drivers out at the airport, picking up tips about how the business works, and before long, we're out there all the time, playing cards, wondering why we aren't making any money. We tell ourselves that drinking coffee will keep us sharp, so we drink coffee and develop a taste for it. Then we're guzzling a giant Styrofoam cup of coffee every few hours, trying not to notice the vague nausea and the rattled nerves. It's all karma. And of course, none of this makes us better cabdrivers.

Of course, we're always planting seeds in the world around us as well. If we're making the world better, we'll get to live in a better world. And most of those seeds will sprout around us, so we'll benefit from them. That's karma too.

There are tragedies being played out around the world all the time. Genocides. Famines. Terrorism. The tsunami in Asia, the drowning of New Orleans, the earthquake in Haiti. The people whose lives were torn apart by these events weren't all suffering from bad karma. They weren't paying for something they did wrong. They were just in the wrong place at the wrong time. But some of them were able to rise above their situations and even help others through, while others were crushed in body and spirit. We can't control the situations we find ourselves in, but we can control our responses to those situations. That's karma.

Of course, for most of us, there are no earthquakes, tsunamis, genocides, famines, or terrorist attacks. Most of our cities will never drown. We are fortunate, but that fortune is not karma, it's only fortune. Are we making the most of our good fortune? Or are we wasting it? We build karma by making the most of what we have, not by waiting for something better to come along.

The good news about karma is that it can change. Our actions are constantly creating new karmic traces, and if we make the effort, we can create a better situation for ourselves. Karmic traces fade away in time. The way to deal with karma is to try to create better karma with our present actions and to try not to worry too much about the effects of the past. We will have good moments and bad. We will succeed, and we will fail. It happens. The Buddha warned against trying to unravel the twisted threads of karma as a way of understanding the events in our lives. There are too many threads to sort out. We couldn't change the past, even if we could understand it. All we can do is try to plant better seeds, now and in the future. And those seeds will grow and come back to us in time.

An important feature of karma is the role of intentions. Accidents and mistakes don't create karma. Intentions do, even when they have no effect at all. Attempted murder, for example, would be as serious as murder. Thinking about murdering someone would also create bad karma, although there must be some good karma in deciding not to act on those thoughts. Making an honest effort to do the right thing creates karma, even when things don't work out. It goes both ways. Merely failing to carry out a plan doesn't negate the karma created by the plan. And the effects of past actions may take many years to work themselves out, so many of us are likely dealing with the traces of thoughts and actions left over from times we can barely remember. On the other hand, our more recent actions are also playing themselves out in the present, so our lives are not being determined by traces of the distant past. Those traces are there, but the most recent influences are the strongest.

So when someone cuts you off in traffic, it's best to just let it go. Don't even think about it. Those revenge fantasies might be fun, but they can't be good for your karma. Even if you don't act out.

The idea of karma is tied up with the doctrine of reincarnation, the belief that we will be reborn into this world again and again. The interests and habits of one lifetime leave a karmic trace for future lives, so someone who is interested in music or athletics might find opportunities to pursue those interests in future lives. Seung Sahn uses as an example the classical musician Mozart. He could have been musically inclined in previous lives and the karma created in those lives led to his rebirth as a great musical prodigy. And the circumstances of his birth made it possible for him to develop those gifts. If he had been reborn under other circumstances, he might never have realized his talent. His gifts and his interests, not his circumstances, were the result of the karma left over from his past lives.

It's fun to think of the way the popular view of karma could play out. Maybe somewhere the current incarnation of Adolf Hitler is wondering why everyone hates him and nothing in his life seems to go the way it should. Or maybe he's just a sad little man who doesn't know why he enjoys pulling the wings off insects.

Or maybe he was reborn as an insect. Over and over. Fun, isn't it?

But that's only speculation. An empty game. An understanding of karma doesn't require a belief in reincarnation at all. It's simply psychology. The workings of our karma can be seen as the result of our own experiences starting from birth. We can't remember our past lives, and we can't do anything about them, so we might as well think of our karma as being only part of our present situation. Then we can work to improve it.

So if you want to work on your karma, get out on those streets and treat the other drivers with courtesy and respect. Be helpful to your passengers and cooperate with the dispatchers. Sow seeds of loving-kindness and wait for them to grow. In time, it will all come back to you.

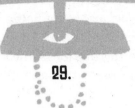

THE END OF THE ROAD

I'm driving down the interstate late at night, south-bound on the lower level, trying to get back downtown in time to load one more fare on 6th Street. There's not much traffic, but I can see taillights ahead, cars slow-ing down, stopping. I pull up in line for a while, then watch an APD cruiser drive down the breakdown lane. Then there's another cruiser, then an ambulance. After a while, the traffic starts up again, very slowly. There's one lane open ahead, a long row of cars behind now, every-one being patient, knowing what's going on. When I get to the accident, there's a Range Rover crushed and flipped over, lying on its roof in the highway, a subcom-pact smashed into it, its windshield and most of the front end gone. The EMTs are standing around, looking shaken, nothing for them to do. A cop is waving the cars by with a flashlight. He's a young guy, maybe a rookie, and he looks like he's going to start crying. I'm trying not to look, but I get a glimpse of a body lying in the space between the cars.

Out in the streets, you see it: people die. Some of them die suddenly, just going home from a club, having a good time, then it's over. You never know what's coming. The way this one looks, the Range Rover didn't make the exit, crashed into the abutment, flipped back onto the highway in front of the hatchback. They never had a chance. It could have been me, driving the cab one moment, my only concern getting back downtown, getting one more fare for the night, and the next moment crushed under a Range Rover, dying instantly.

When someone we know dies, it's a shock, especially when it's someone young, someone we thought would live forever. In other cases, it's someone who's been suffering, who's had a full life, and there's a sense of relief that their pain has ended. Then again, sometimes someone we don't even know dies and their story affects us as if we'd known them. And we grieve for them.

Grief isn't something we can just ignore. We can say that grief comes from attachment, and we just need to let go of that attachment, but it's a hard thing to do. It's natural to feel grief for loved ones who pass away, but we shouldn't be attached to our grief. We shouldn't let it pull us down. The dead don't want us to suffer for them. Personally, I don't want anyone grieving over me. I'd like to be remembered, but not with sadness. I'd prefer an Irish wake, a celebration of my life, with no sadness at all.

And I'd rather it didn't happen for a long, long time.

I once knew a woman who went into a severe depression over the death—not of a friend or loved one—but her dog. The dog had lived a wonderful life, had been well-treated, and lived to the age of thirteen. All the other Great Danes in dog heaven must have been jealous. The woman's depression went on for months, and just got worse when she tried to explain why she was so upset about it. I'm sure the dog didn't want her to suffer like that.

And our friends and relatives don't want us to suffer either.

Most of the time, we manage not to think about death. You could say it's the elephant in the room of our life. We're all whistling past that graveyard, and we get pretty good at it. But when it strikes close to you, it makes you think. I drive past the wreck on the highway, and suddenly I'm not thinking about getting downtown. I'm thinking about friends who died over the years. And I'm thinking about myself, wondering when my time will come.

A few years ago, I was riding a motorcycle and came up behind a car at a light with a vanity plate that read: *Brian*. I got this strange feeling, thinking this was a bumper with my name on it, and I'd better be careful. When the light changed, I dropped back, let him get a few blocks on me. Just to be sure.

Cabdriving is one of the most dangerous occupations. From time to time, a driver will be killed in a robbery or some kind of altercation. Or a wreck. It doesn't happen often, not in Austin, but it makes you think. Every so often, there's a trip with a passenger who might be trouble, someone you wish you hadn't picked up. And that makes you think.

Zen is a practice for the living. And death is a central part of life. By avoiding the thought of death, we take some of the meaning from our lives. Part of Zen practice is to put that meaning back. Death is certain, and it can come at any time, so we should appreciate our lives. We should use the time we have wisely and practice diligently. Death provides an incentive to develop our practice while we can.

If we were going to live forever, there would be plenty of time. We aren't. There isn't. The road doesn't go on forever. The party does end.

Death is a prime example of impermanence. Everything passes away in time, and we do too. It's all ashes to plant food in this world. To understand life, we have to face death. In some practices, students are urged to perform guided meditations focusing on the reality of their own deaths. The idea is to use the reality of death to help develop an active moment-to-moment appreciation of daily life.

Reincarnation and rebirth of some kind are fundamental concepts in all forms of Buddhism. It is claimed by some that one cannot practice Buddhism without accepting the principle of reincarnation. Not everyone agrees. One view is that the Buddha merely accepted the prevailing belief in reincarnation that already existed in India, and adapted it along with the workings of karma to fit his own system. On the other hand, legend says that, when he attained enlightenment, the Buddha remembered his five hundred previous incarnations and saw the patterns that united them, all leading to his eventual enlightenment.

Buddhists have held a wide range of attitudes toward life after death. The Shin school, also known as Pure Land Buddhism, teaches that followers who obey the precepts and lead deeply spiritual lives will be reborn in another realm that seems very much like the Christian version of heaven. On the other hand, there is evidence that early Christians and other Israelites believed in a form of reincarnation as well.

In Zen, there is little speculation about the nature of rebirth beyond its involvement with karma, and the meditation practice itself does not require a belief in rebirth. There's a sense that living mindfully moment to moment is enough. The practice may lead to a belief in reincarnation, but it doesn't have to begin there. Suzuki-roshi, for example, describes death as being like a small stream of water rejoining a river, an image that leaves the possibility of personal rebirth open and unresolved.

In Tibetan Buddhism, on the other hand, death and rebirth are central to everyday practice. One approach is to overcome the fear of death by facing it squarely. Monks have been known to drink from human skulls and play human bones as horns. Another practice is to sleep in Himalayan graveyards littered with unburied corpses. Familiarity breeds a healthy contempt for death. Or it leads to years of therapy.

The Tibetan views of life and death are given in the *Bardo Thödol*, better known as *The Tibetan Book of the Dead*. It was written in the eighth century by Padmasambhava, the founder of Tibetan Buddhism. It provides a series of instructions to aid the deceased in the journey through the *bardos*, or transitional states, between death and rebirth. The instructions are meant to be spoken into the ears of the dead to guide them through the period between lives.

In the Tibetan system, there are four bardos. The first is our actual life, from birth to the moment of physical death. That is followed by a period of several days in which the spirit stays with the body. Then the spirit enters a period of bright, clear light. After this, the workings of karma operate to guide the spirit to the conditions of its next incarnation.

In each of the bardos, there is opportunity for awakening. The best opportunity is in this life, and we should focus our energies on this practice, but it is also possible for the deceased to achieve enlightenment in the other bardos and to escape the circle of life and death. It is also possible for the souls to pass into other realms. According to tradition, there are six realms, including a hell realm and a realm of the gods that seems like the Pure Land of Shin.

Or we get to come back and try again.

While *The Tibetan Book of the Dead* describes events in a context familiar to Tibetans, people of other cultures would have similar experiences but in a context familiar to them. Westerners might experience the bardo with Judeo-Christian figures and symbolism. Or some other themes might be played out.

Surprisingly, there is some evidence to support the possibility of reincarnation. For one thing, there have been numerous reports of children who claim to have detailed memories of a past life, and in some cases their versions of events have been studied and verified at least in part. Hypnosis has also been used to help adults recover details of their past lives. While there has been a great deal of out-and-out fraud, some serious researchers have been able to produce verifiable results from this method. For example, one woman described in detail her life in an ancient city in the Middle East. At the time, her report was discounted because no such city was known to have existed. Later, however, the ruins of the city were found, and the site held a number of the features she had described. While this is not definite proof of reincarnation, it suggests interesting possibilities. And raises the hairs on the back of my neck.

Further evidence for reincarnation comes from the Tulku tradition of Tibet. When a great master prepares for death, he will tell his disciples the general area where his rebirth will take place. A few years after his death, the disciples will go to the area to find him. They will search for children of the right age who have an active interest in spiritual matters, select the most likely candidates, and then give them a series of tests to select the Tulku, or true incarnation of the master. These include selecting the personal possessions of the master from among a large group of objects and picking out the master's close friends from among a group of strangers. This method is claimed to produce a clear choice—the true incarnation of the deceased master. The Dalai Lama is one of the masters chosen in this way. This process is depicted in the Martin Scorsese film about the Dalai Lama, *Kundun*.

In the West, there is a strong desire for life to continue after death, whether in the form of reincarnation or in the Christian concept of heaven. Ironically, the Eastern view is that reincarnation is a curse, an unending sentence. Life, after all, involves suffering, and we are condemned to suffer not only in this life, but in future lives as well. The instructions in *The Tibetan Book of the Dead* are meant to help the newly dead to avoid rebirth, to escape the endless cycle of birth and death.

According to legend, the Buddha's enlightenment was so complete that he was never reincarnated. He left the cycle of life and death behind when he died. It is believed (by some) that he and all the other fully enlightened buddhas of history live on in a realm of absolute bliss called the buddha fields. This is, however, pure myth. There haven't been any posthumous messages from the Buddha.

And no one's waiting for any.

Driving away from the scene I think for a moment about the people in the accident. Where are they now? Are they standing before the gates of heaven, trying to explain themselves? Or in a bardo, trying to grasp what is happening to them? Or are they only gone, sleeping the big sleep? I push the thought from my mind. It's this moment that matters. And I'd better pay attention to the traffic or I'll find out about death sooner than I want to.

Now I'm back downtown, loading three college kids going up to campus, getting back into the action. Already the thought of the accident out on the highway is fading. I don't have to think about death tonight. It doesn't help to speculate. The truth is, we don't know what will come when this life ends, so beyond facing death honestly and openly, there isn't much we can do about it. All we can do is take this life moment by moment, appreciating each one as if it were our last. Because you never know. It could be.

METAPHYSICAL ME

Now that we've seen how the essentials of Zen practice, like mindfulness and the precepts, work in real life, it's time to look at some of the ideas behind Buddhism. Don't be afraid. We'll keep it light. We don't want anyone to get a headache from any of this. It's hard to drive with a headache.

When the Buddha attained enlightenment under the bodhi tree, the insight that sparked his realization was that everything was connected to everything else. He was sitting there watching the morning star rise in the sky, and he realized that he and the morning star were just the same. There was no dualism in the world. That one insight set his mind free and led him to a whole new way of seeing the world. It was like a jigsaw puzzle that seemed impossible until one key piece was found and everything fell into place.

Modern Western philosophy begins with the idea of dualism. This practice of drawing basic distinctions was developed by René Descartes and others. According to dualism, everything can be divided into separate, individual objects. The most basic distinction for Descartes was between mind and body. Others include self and other, good and bad, right and wrong. Our sense of the world is based on drawing distinctions between different objects and different ideas. We give each a name and a separate identity. And we think of it as distinct from everything else in the world. That's dualism.

But is the world dualistic, or are we?

Zen teaches that everything is connected, part of a whole that is greater than the sum of its parts. All distinctions are arbitrary—and wrong. The distinctions are only psychology. If we could see clearly enough, we would see that everything fits together into one seamless whole. This is one way of thinking about the famous lines from the Heart Sutra, "Form is emptiness; emptiness is form." Form defines the emptiness around it, and the emptiness defines the form. One without the other would be meaningless.

Remember the scene in *Zen in the Art of Archery* in which Eugen Herrigel is told to become one with the bow. This means to see beyond dualism to the real nature of archery, the unity of archer, bow, arrow, and target. Then let the arrow find its own way to the target. When Herrigel is able to let go of his dualistic understanding, he can split the target with the arrow.

It's also like driving a cab on a busy night. After a while, you're just out there, flowing through the city, one with the cab, the streets, the city, the world. The distractions fade away. You lose yourself in what you're doing, and you forget to draw those distinctions for a while.

According to Zen, dualism is only a delusion, an interpretation we put on the world around us to help us make sense of it. And it helps. It's a practical way of looking at things. But when we get too caught up in it, it turns into a handicap. We wind up living in a world of our own making—and missing the world as it really is.

The greatest delusion of all is the idea of a separate self, a concrete entity cut off from everything else. All those thoughts, opinions, memories, likes, and dislikes, they're only empty psychology. That inner monologue that goes on from minute to minute is only a distraction. Everything we think of as a separate self is only emptiness. Zen practice is a way of peeling away the layers of the self so we can see through it. That's what we've been doing in *Dharma Road*. Peeling away those layers, searching for our true nature. Once we see through the self, the world itself is different. We're no longer looking at it; we're in it, part of it. We are the world.

In the world according to Zen, everything is fully connected, intertwined. Mind and body are the same. You and I are not different. Earth and sky are only parts of something larger. Every distinction is only a coin with heads on one side, tails on the other. Heads and tails are not different. In Zen there is no dualism. And all we have to do is see deeply enough within ourselves to see that dualism is only a delusion.

Imagine yourself driving down a stretch of Mopac Expressway, doing about twenty in rush hour traffic. The sun is going down, and the traffic is one mass of headlights coming toward you from the other side and another mass of taillights in front, moving with you. Rush hour is running late tonight: the expressway's jammed in both directions, the frontage roads, the overpasses, the intersections—everything's moving, but nothing's moving very fast. You're feeling good, in control, got the radio on, some nice blues in the air. You're here in your cab, and there's everyone else outside. But that's only part of the story. You're also just a part of a stream of traffic moving down a four-lane highway, and you're not really separate from the stream. It just seems that way.

There's a helicopter overhead with one of those traffic reporters who tell you you're in a jam after it's too late to do much about it. From up there, we're all just streams of headlights mindlessly following each other around, forming the same patterns over and over. And from farther away, the helicopter is just another part of the traffic.

You want to change lanes, but there's no space on your right, so you slow down, look for an opening. The traffic ahead pulls away a little, and the cars flow around you. Finally, there's an opening and you pull into it, match speed with the traffic. Are you separate from the other drivers, or are you just part of the flow?

Some people think Zen denies individuality and free will, but that's not true. We still live in the world, and we always have choices, but there are also limits. Getting on the expressway, we have to merge with the cars to the left, then merge again to make it into the second lane. When the traffic ahead slows down, we slow down with it. We can choose an exit, but we have to maneuver to get there, and we have to stop when the light at the cross street turns red. From our individual points of view, it seems like we're exercising our free will, doing whatever we want. But we're wrong. We're only choosing our actions from a limited number of options. And everything in our lives is that way. The traffic is just an example. A metaphor.

In the words of composer John Cage: "We are as free as birds. Only the birds aren't free."

When doing zazen, the interior monologue that narrates most of our lives slows down and fades away. We stop analyzing the world and interpreting our place in it. For a while, we are free from all our dualistic ways. And in time we can see the world in a fresh new way. Practicing mindfulness, whether driving down Mopac in the cab or aiming an arrow at a distant target or doing kinhin on a city sidewalk, we put the dualism away for a while, take the world as it really is. And we take ourselves as we really are. Just for a while, we are completely consumed in what we are doing, with nothing left over. We find that there is no need for a narrator to tell us what we're doing. Or who we are. We take ourselves as we really are. That's Zen.

When we see our true nature, we see that we're not all separate, completely isolated from each other. Our dualistic ideas drop away. We see that we're all part of something larger, just cabs in the slow-moving stream of traffic out on Mopac tonight.

Or at least that's what I've heard. I haven't actually seen it. Not yet. But sometimes, just for a moment out in the traffic, I can almost feel it. And sitting in the airport line when it's quiet and there's nothing moving, I can stare off into the darkness through the swarms of insects around the streetlights at the high clouds that float across the moon and I can lose myself, just take it all in and be free for a while. As free as the birds.

MAPS AND WORDS

We all carry around a map of our surroundings in our minds. For most people, it's just a general sketch of the way things go together, the places they go, the streets they use. For cabdrivers, the maps are more detailed with shortcuts and local landmarks, frequent destinations. They might include the details of large apartment complexes, the names of clubs and restaurants downtown. When I hear the name of a street, I'll remember the people I've picked up there, people I've dropped off, things that happened with them. Sometimes I'll remember a regular rider who lived there awhile ago. Or I'll have some connection with the street, something from before I was a cabdriver. It's all in that mental map I'm carrying around.

We have other maps. They range from a star map of the galaxy on down to the layout of our homes, the way things are arranged in our yards. On every scale, there's a map to help us get around. And we have diagrams, working models of everything in our world. I can imagine a schematic diagram of the cab I drive, floor plans and elevations of my house, maps of the weather systems that come through. Our whole world is represented in our minds by an endless series of representations.

They're only maps.

In my mind, most of the streets in Austin are laid out on a grid. They run east-west or north-south. A few of them run in a diagonal, or circle around, or follow the route of a creek. I remember those in relation to the larger grid. A street comes up, and right away I focus on the part of town, on the geometry of the main streets, on the grid. If I had to, I could sit down with a pen and a really large sheet of paper and draw a detailed map of the city.

Of course, it wouldn't be accurate. The streets don't really run east-west or north-south. That's a convention to make directions easier to understand. Like most cities, Austin wasn't planned, it grew little by little over the course of about 170 years. Most neighborhoods are laid out in some kind of a grid, with blocks aligned to follow one of the major roads, most of which run more or less north-south or east-west. But sometimes I get home late at night to my own east-west street and see the moon coming up in what should be the northeast, and it's a reminder that the map is just an approximation of the way things are. It's not reality.

Language is another kind of map. It contains a logical structure that mirrors our ideas about the nature of the world. And our ideas about the world in turn are shaped by our language. When we think about the world, we usually think in words. Language is dualistic—it reinforces our sense of separation from the world. It works to divide this from that, and to separate us from everything else. Language reinforces a view of the world that helps us to deal with it on a day-to-day basis but keeps us from ever truly understanding it.

Language is one of the most important differences between humans and other animals. Without it, we'd still be living in caves. But, as scientist and philosopher Alfred Korzybski famously said, "The map is not the territory." Language is only a mental map of the world, and it doesn't do justice to the reality. It's not reality either.

Much of Western philosophy consists of disagreements over the meaning of words. Most people are familiar with the question posed by Bishop George Berkeley, "If a tree falls in the forest and no one is around to hear it, does it make a sound?" Berkeley was making an important point about the subjective nature of reality, but the question can be reduced to a debate over the meaning of the word "sound." If sound is merely the vibration of the air, then the answer is yes. If sound is its perception, the answer is no. What do you mean by the word *sound?*

But there's another way to view the world. According to Seung Sahn, "Zen teaching simply means not attaching to language." Words only point to reality: when we perceive the world as it is portrayed in language, we are not perceiving it directly. When we let go of the language, we can go beyond the dualistic view and experience it as it truly is.

In one of the Buddha's most famous sermons, delivered on Vulture Peak, he sat for a while in silence and then simply held up a flower. This was a demonstration of direct experience of reality as opposed to conceptual experience. It may not have been one of the Buddha's most successful sermons—only one of those present became enlightened—but it remains a poignant example of his teaching. And it was his answer to the philosophers who speculate in great detail about the world around them.

At one time in China, monks practiced by memorizing and reciting the sutras of Buddhism. Volumes of them. Seung Sahn tells a story about the greatest sutra master of his time, who had mastered every sutra ever written. People would come from far away to ask for his advice. They would tell him about their problem, and he would recite for them the sutra that would solve that problem. One day, a strange nun came to him and refused to listen to any of his sutras. She wanted to hear his own speech, his own words. She was asking about his true nature. And he was speechless. He knew nothing about his own true nature. After that, he abandoned his attachment to the sutras and began to experience the world as it was. In time, he became a great master.

We haven't discussed koan study. Koans are questions that seem to be only nonsense but have a deeper meaning. What is the sound of one hand clapping? Well, I'll be honest: I have no idea what the sound of one hand clapping is. Koan study is a little too advanced for hardworking cabdrivers like us. We're just beginners, after all. Monks can spend months or even years meditating on a koan, and we don't have time for that. But it's safe to say that after years of koan study, language begins to break down and the world itself begins to shine through.

It's important to read about Zen and to listen to dharma talks. But this is only language. Zen is not something to read about. It's something to live. In the end, there are no road maps of the Eightfold Freeway, no tourist guides. If you enjoy reading *Dharma Road*, you might go on to read some other books about Buddhism. You might read Shunryu Suzuki and Seung Sahn or some of the books by the current incarnation of the Dalai Lama. And you might go on from there to read the sutras of the Buddha and the writings of Dogen Zenji and the other great teachers through the centuries. There's a reading list at the back of this book (kind of a casual bibliography) if you need help picking something out. Stop by the library or your favorite bookstore and browse for a while. But all these are only words. Zen is meant to be practiced. If you only read about Zen, you will never truly understand it.

If you only read about life, you won't understand that either.

So if it's a slow day and you're going out to the airport to sit in line for a couple hours, bring something to read. But don't just read about Zen. While you're out there, you might want to walk away from the cab lot for a few minutes and stand out there in the grass with the oleanders and the crickets and feel the wind around you and the sun on your face.

That's Zen too.

GOD HIDES IN THE TRAFFIC

Four in the morning in the airport line, I'm sitting on the hood of the cab, staring off into the overcast sky. There's a swarm of insects buzzing around each of the streetlights. Not much else is moving. Tumbleweeds could roll through here anytime now. There's a short line of cabs in the lot with the drivers leaning on the fenders, looking discouraged. A time like this, you do a lot of thinking. At least I do.

One thing I'm thinking is that I should have worked harder in the afternoon. Then I wouldn't have to be out here waiting for one more fare so I can make my lease payment.

I'm also thinking about the big questions. Who are we and why are we here? Who is god and what does he want from us? Or: What the hell does he want from me? You know, the big questions.

Zen is a practice, a way of living. There are some instructions and activities, steps to take on a path to realization. There's not much room for speculation in

Zen. There's no dogma, no metaphysics. There are no stories about creation or how an all-powerful god carries out a plan for our lives. The big questions are only a distraction from the real work of spiritual growth, so we ignore them. Most of the time, anyway.

Sometimes—four in the morning in the airport line, for example—it's fun to speculate about the true nature of the world around us. Many cosmologists now believe that ours is but one of an infinite number of universes in what is called the megaverse. Universes are constantly being formed, and each has its own set of physical laws. Most of the universes either quickly collapse or fail to evolve any kind of structures like the ones we see around us. Almost all of them are lifeless and downright weird. And we have no way of ever reaching out to any of the other universes, even to the extent of verifying that they exist.

See, that was fun. It's really just speculation—there's not much real science behind it—but the cosmologists seem to take it seriously. Some of them, anyway. And it's four in the morning, so we might as well have a little fun with it.

Actually, the idea of the megaverse was developed to answer a difficult question. Everything in our world, from the basic physical laws and constants to the climate and mineral content of the earth, seems designed to make life as we know it a reality. It's all an extreme long shot. The megaverse is a way of explaining that without resorting to a version of intelligent design. It avoids the question of god.

Which do you think is more far-fetched, the megaverse or god?

Buddhism is often called a religion without a god. Or a nontheistic religion. Since we're taking on the weighty questions, we really ought to think about god. Or God, if we're talking about the Christian God.

The Buddha was not a god. He was a man, like any of us. Even after his awakening, he was just a mortal man, making his way in the world like everyone else, but doing it with a greater understanding. In some traditions, the Buddha is worshipped, but that's not the idea behind the religion. The Buddha doesn't really grant favors or bless marriages. And he never wanted to be worshipped. It's the idea of buddhahood that is being worshipped, the example he set for us. The man himself is still only a man.

But that doesn't mean there is no god, only that the Buddha isn't one.

The religions of the world have a lot to say about the nature of god, what he (or she, or it) wants us to do, how he wants us to do it. Countless wars have been fought over these issues, and the strife goes on today. All these interpretations are only speculations.

There's not much room for speculation in Zen. It's all experience. Practice. Here's a metaphor. You go into a tall building and find that the elevator is out. You've heard there's a great view of the city from the roof, twenty floors up, and you really wanted to see it. Should you stand around in the lobby, speculating about the view, wondering what it's like? Hoping someone comes along to fix the elevator? Or should you take the stairs? Buddhists take the stairs, one step at a time.

Many people, including many practicing Christians, don't really believe in any of the usual anthropomorphic conceptions of god. They think of god as a force in the universe, more like an underlying intelligence, a deeper meaning behind the chaos of life. They see the mythic elements of Christianity as a representation of a deeper reality too subtle for us to grasp. And they see heaven and hell simply as states of mind or being that continue after death.

Academic theologians tend to agree with these views. In modern theology, god is not seen as separate from the world or from ourselves. For example, there's Bishop George Berkeley's view that our world is really an idea in the mind of god. This doesn't fit with the idea of a superhuman god who watches us from above, rewarding or punishing us for our actions. Berkeley's god is the ground that includes everything in our world. And ourselves. This is much closer to the Buddhist conception of the sacred.

Thomas Moore is a former Catholic monk and the author of *The Soul's Religion* and many other books on modern spirituality. He notes that although he writes about religion, he rarely writes directly about god because he thinks of god as unnamable and, to some extent, unknowable. His solution to this is to look for god in everyday life, in the little miracles of the mundane world. So he looks for signs of god on the same streets I drive on as I try to find myself.

Is this getting a little heavy? I know. This started out as a lighthearted look at Zen and cabdriving, and now we're going into theology. Life's like that sometimes. Don't worry. This won't be on the test for your hack license. Besides, we're talking about god here. Deal with it.

A number of Christians have embraced Buddhist practice, in part as a way of deepening their own Christian practice. The two can be complementary. Monk and philosopher Thomas Merton studied Zen and wrote extensively about the similarities between Buddhist and Christian practices. More recently, Father Thomas Keating has explored a range of monastic practices that closely resemble Zen practices. Thomas Moore also embraces Zen along with his Christian background. And it works the other way too. Vietnamese Zen master Thich Nhat Hanh was exposed to Christian ideals through his work in the peace movement during the Vietnam War. In his book *Living Buddha, Living Christ*, he describes some of the similarities between the practices. For example, the Christian idea of the Holy Spirit is similar to the idea of Buddha nature, the essence that permeates all existence. He also says that on the shelf in his meditation chamber, he keeps a statue of Buddha and another of Jesus Christ. For inspiration.

The claim that Buddhism is atheistic is based on a limited and simplistic concept of god. And of Buddhism. There is nothing limited about either Buddhism or god. The Buddhist view of the world includes most of the attributes of god without creating a dualistic idea of a being separate from ourselves and from our lives. There is no separate being who controls our existence and destiny. But there is an underlying reality, a deeper meaning to our lives that could be called godlike. And it's up to us to explore that and to include it in our lives.

Some cabdrivers have plastic statues of Jesus Krazy Glued to their dashboards. Some of them do it to remind themselves of what is really important in their lives. Others just think it helps bring in the tips. I don't have a plastic Jesus or a bobblehead Buddha on my dashboard. I don't think I need anything like that. They are only more distractions. I'm looking for god out there in the world, in the sunset sky over the interstate, in the neon shining on the rain-slicked streets after midnight.

And I'm looking inside as well. Just to see.

THE LIGHTS COME ON
[OR AT LEAST BLINK]

The interstate is clogged, the evening traffic in both directions barely moving. The ramps, the access roads, the overpasses, they're all crowded, moving slowly. There's movement: cars change lanes, change back, wind up about where they started. The drivers glare at each other, flash their headlights, sound the horn. Some of them pound their steering wheel in frustration. No one's really going anywhere, but they're all trying real hard.

One car pulls out of line, first into the breakdown lane, then onto the soft grass of the shoulder. A little at a time, it climbs a slope to the top of a ridge separating the highway and the frontage road. It stops there and looks out over the mass of traffic below, feeling free.

It's a cab. Number 119.

The hope of breaking free from this world of delusion has always been the main attraction of Buddhism.

It was true for the crowds attending the Buddha's lectures, and it's true for the twenty-first-century cabdrivers sitting zazen in cabstands and parking lots around the world. It's an elusive goal, but what other goals are there? And besides, it's not really a goal at all. Only the path really matters.

One of the problems with the idea of enlightenment is that it's impossible to describe. It's like describing a sunset to a blind man: words do not suffice. It's the ego falling away, leaving the truth behind. A wider perspective on the world. A state of perpetual bliss. Or simply lasting peace of mind.

Enlightenment is seeing our true nature, the truth behind the appearances and the delusions.

It's redemption without all the sin.

Don't ask me. I'm just the cabdriver. This part of the road you'll have to discover for yourself.

Zen practice doesn't require acts of faith. The practice is geared toward moral, ethical living and steady spiritual progress. You only have to believe what you experience for yourself. The only faith required is the belief that it is possible to gain some kind of awakening from the limitations of our human condition.

After his enlightenment, when the Buddha went out to teach others, he was clearly changed. People were immediately drawn to him just by his appearance.

He was asked, "Are you a god?"

"No," he said.

"Are you a man?"

"No," he said again.

"Then what are you?"

"I am awake."

When the Buddha taught, there were records kept of the number of listeners who became enlightened at each sermon. It seems to have been a common experience. Maybe it was easier then. It was a simpler time with fewer distractions. Perhaps it was the personal power of the Buddha, or his talent as an orator. Legend has it that many beings had come to the edge of enlightenment over many lifetimes and were waiting only for a great master to guide them for the final step. Over the course of history, there are many stories of students becoming enlightened just hearing a word from a master, or seeing something that hit them the right way. It seems to be harder now. It takes years of diligent practice, and it may not happen at all.

Here's my favorite enlightenment story, told by Seung Sahn. A monk was carrying an old wooden bucket filled with water. It was a clear night with a full moon, and the moon was reflected on the surface of the water. As he walked, the bottom of the bucket sprung a leak, and the water drained from the bucket. Watching the moon's reflection fall down through the bucket, the monk was enlightened. I can just picture that moon falling, the smile lighting up the monk's face.

In most stories of enlightenment, students are prepared for the experience by years of practice and have arrived at the edge of the abyss. At this point, only a little nudge, like the image of the moon falling through the bottom of a leaking bucket, will be enough. In one story, after the Buddha's death, his faithful companion Ananda was to attend a conference that would agree on the sutras to be accepted as the Buddha's original teachings. Since he had heard all the Buddha's lectures, his presence was critical. However, the conference was only for the enlightened, and Ananda had not yet attained enlightenment. As the time neared, he meditated frantically, trying to qualify for the conference, but he just wasn't able to do it. Finally, just as the conference was opening, he gave up, told himself it was hopeless. And in that moment of surrender, he felt the veils of delusion fall away and at last he was enlightened.

And then there's Hui Neng, an illiterate peasant who had no training in the dharma. He made his living by carrying firewood from the hillsides into the town. He was enlightened upon hearing a monk recite just one line of the Diamond Sutra and became the Sixth Patriarch of Chinese Zen.

While the awakenings of historical figures such as the Buddha, Ananda, and Hui Neng are usually described as sudden and dramatic, a more modern view is the idea that awakening occurs in steps, beginning with brief glimpses and progressing through more dramatic realizations to the final state of total enlightenment. This theme is explored by Seung Sahn in *The Compass of Zen*. The title itself refers to the degrees of enlightenment experienced with diligent practice.

When the Buddha was enlightened, he said he finally realized that all beings are already enlightened. This means that the essence of enlightenment—known as Buddha nature—is within each of us, but it is obscured by our delusions and preconceptions. Our opinions. Our likes and dislikes. Our practice is to clear away the debris of our lives and see through to the truth within. This view is often symbolized by the image of the sun emerging from behind a veil of clouds.

In Soto Zen, enlightenment is downplayed in favor of day-to-day, minute-by-minute practice. It is said that sitting zazen is itself a form of enlightenment. This attitude goes back to Dogen, the founder of Soto Zen, who stressed the importance of everyday practice without focusing on the goal of enlightenment. As Suzuki-roshi explained, "It's not that satori is unimportant, but it's not the part of Zen that needs to be stressed." While diligent practice may lead to an enlightenment experience, there are no guarantees. The practice is its own reward.

There is a saying, "If you meet the Buddha on the road, kill him." This refers to the danger that students of Zen will become attached to the idea of enlightenment. As long as enlightenment is something outside the self, a goal to strive for, the practice itself will suffer. The Buddha you meet on the road—or the image of enlightenment as a goal—is something extra that just gets in the way of day-to-day practice.

In my own case, I'm resigned to the idea that I might have to be content with some peace of mind, a decent rebirth, and a shot at the real thing in a future life. I've wasted time, been caught up in delusions, acted foolishly. I've messed up on some of the precepts. Well, quite a few of them, at one time or another. I've practiced zazen sporadically, sometimes not at all. And on top of that, I have a short attention span that makes progress difficult. As excuses go, they're not bad. And if I have to, I'll think of some more.

Then again, you never know.

On a Tuesday night, around ten o'clock, for just a few moments, I become enlightened.

I'm driving down Mopac in a soft rain, the first in weeks. The roads are slick from the motor oil raised by the rain, and there's not enough water to wash the oil away. I know the start of a rain is the worst time to be driving. I'm taking it slow, no hurry at all, heading downtown.

A call comes out on the radio, a fare on 38th Street. It's probably Seton Hospital, maybe a short run on a voucher, but that doesn't matter. On a Tuesday night, any fare will do. The exit is just ahead, so I take the call. It's at the medical office building next to Seton. I pull into the right lane and make the exit.

The exit runs down a ramp to a stop sign. I wait there for a few cars to clear and then pull out and cross the westbound lane to make the left turn onto 38th. As I pass the median divider and start the turn, the rear wheels break free, and the car begins to slide sound-lessly along the road, just hydroplaning away, the cab spinning slowly, completely beyond my control. I try the brake, very softly, then harder, try to steer into the skid, then the other way, looking for something that will help. Nothing does.

And I'm sliding, alert but helpless, just watching through the windshield as the world goes by in slow motion. A yield sign, the trunk of a live oak covered with vines, a couple of orange pylons, all of it out of context, just pieces of a world going by, like a dream about cab-driving. I'm taking it all in, accepting it, not fighting for control. There's a guardrail, a telephone pole hung with colored flyers, a no-left-turn sign, and there's nothing I can do but watch it happen, pay attention as it goes by.

Then a rear wheel hits the curb on the median, bounces hard, the front wheels dig in, the trunk pops open, and the motor stalls, all in a half second and I'm sitting there, thinking, *That's what it must be like. Enlightenment.* A mixture of adrenaline and helplessness, and more. A lot more. Attention. Acceptance. Taking the world just as it is, not backing away, not trying to hide from it. Not trying to control it. Enlightenment.

It's not really enlightenment.

It's just a moment on the road. Maybe a glimpse, a quick look at the world as it is. Or just a jolt of excitement, an illusion of enlightenment. What it might be like. A Zen master would be able to clear this up for me, but I'm on my own out here, so I'll take this as a sign that there's hope for me yet.

It's best to have a little faith.

I sit there in the eastbound lane for a minute, facing the wrong direction, not caring at all. A car pulls up, stops. The driver asks if I need any help.

"No," I tell him. "I'm just fine, thank you. I'm just going to sit here a minute, enjoy the evening." He drives away, shaking his head, probably wondering about my sanity.

Finally, I get out and slam the trunk, take a look around. It's a beautiful night, soft mist in the air, lit up yellow by the lights up on Mopac. The cars up there make a hissing sound on the wet pavement. There's an ozone smell in the air. It looks like I did two and a half turns. That's a nine hundred. There's a spiral trail in the oil slick that coats the road. It looks like a double helix. I'm about a hundred feet past the intersection, maybe a little more. Not a bad one to drive away from. I get the car going, make a slow U-turn, head off to load my next fare. But inside there's a part of me thinking: *That was fun. I want to try that again.*

And it's true. I do want to try that again. Not the out-of-control, bad-driving part, but the glimpse of the world-as-it-is part. I want to keep practicing, studying, doing zazen, being mindful in the cab, getting myself ready. Preparing myself for the next realization. Maybe the next time, I can have a lasting insight, something that will stay with me. Something that will light up the road ahead of me like some kind of psychic headlight. Or light the spirit inside me like fog lamps working in the haze.

Maybe one day I can do it without almost wrecking the cab.

NEW YEAR'S EVE

New Year's Eve.

For cabdrivers, it's the night of nights. The night we look forward to all year long. The one we'll talk about through the coming year. The night that separates the focused, live-in-the-moment, eyes-on-the-road cabdrivers from the stressed-out wannabes.

And it's a great night to make some money, get caught up on those lease payments.

It's the cabdrivers' equivalent of a Jackie Chan movie. Nonstop action. And if Jackie gets distracted, he'll take some hard punches. We'll take some too.

There's something about New Year's. It's a fresh start. We can clear away everything that went wrong in the last year and try again. This time, we'll get it right. Everyone has a list of New Year's resolutions. We're all going to lose weight, stop smoking, start working out, learn to play the guitar, learn quantum mechanics. Become enlightened. There's a sense of a new beginning, the idea that anything is possible. I like that idea. I want to believe.

Really, it's always New Years. Any time you want, you can put aside the baggage from your past and start over. It's not easy, but it's there. Like they say, today is the first day of the rest of your life. This moment is the first moment of the rest of your life. And you can treat each moment that way, just go on seeing the world with a full heart and clear eyes, never looking back, living that moment the best you can. That's Zen, right there. Zen is New Year's Eve, all the time.

There's a rhythm to New Year's Eve. It starts in the early evening. Everyone's headed downtown for the big party on 6th Street. You go out to streets with names like Lonesome Valley Trail and Mountainclimb Drive to pick people up and take them downtown. At first, you're taking them to the restaurants. Later, they're going straight to the bars. The people are cheerful, friendly. They're looking forward to a big night on the town. You try to drop them off without getting caught in the downtown traffic. You don't want to get bogged down, distracted. Then you go out and do it again.

And again. And again.

At midnight, I'm coming into downtown on South 1st with a young couple in the back. I can hear the *pop-pop-pop* of fireworks, horns blaring, people yelling. I pull onto the bridge over Lady Bird Lake, and I'm on the bridge when I hear an explosion on my left. There's a shower of white light, then orange, then purple. A fireworks display, right out over the water. The traffic stops, and everyone on the bridge gets out of their cars to watch. The city comes alive in the flashing light.

Boom!

People run between the cars, coming out from every-where to see. Couples are kissing. Someone's dancing down the sidewalk, making up a rhythm as he goes. Six or eight people are standing on the side of the bridge, yelling, "Happy New Year!" together out into the open air.

Boom!

The lakeshores are lit a ghostly gray from the fall-ing embers. A diesel is crossing the lake on the railroad bridge to the west and the engineer leans on the horn. Smoke drifts across the water.

Boom!

A crowd is forming on the bridge. Everyone is smil-ing and happy, their hearts wide open. *Ooh*ing and *aah*ing at the spectacle. I sit on a fender and watch the cascades of light in the sky with a smile on my face and no thoughts at all in my head.

Boom! Boom! Boom!

The display ends too soon, with a furious run of light and sound, and everyone cheers madly. Then we all get in our cars and wait. Finally, the traffic starts to move. I drop the couple on Guadalupe and load another cou-ple, heading over to Shoal Creek Boulevard. I'm back on it.

After midnight, the tide shifts. Now people are try-ing to get home. Some of them are excited, on top of the world. Some of them are trashed, pissed off. As it gets later, most of them are just worn out. Most of the trips are from downtown out to a house or an apartment. After each trip, I turn around, race downtown, do it all again. The bars close at two, but there are so many people in the streets, it hardly matters. I turn them over as fast as I can, stay focused. They won't be out here tomorrow.

There's a wreck on the interstate. Fender benders here and there. A fight in a parking lot on Lavaca. Bad drivers. Angry pedestrians. Rude passengers. Really bad drunks. And sloppy, sad drunks. It's a new year, but the world hasn't changed.

And there are people smiling, singing in the streets. Kissing on the corners. Talking to each other and listening. Helping each other out in the traffic. Thanking the cabdriver and throwing in a generous tip. Like I said, the world hasn't changed.

The world hasn't changed, and we haven't changed either. But we can. Not all at once just because it's a new year and we want it to be a better year, but because we are free. Every moment, we have it within us to turn a corner and start anew. We can look at the world with clear eyes and open hearts, and we can look inside ourselves to see who we really are. It isn't easy. Dharma Road is a long, hard drive. It takes commitment and dedication. But we can all do it. We only have to try.

New Year's can be a great time to take that first big step. Right now would be a better time. If it helps, just pretend that it's New Year's. For you, it will be.

Around four, I drop a young couple at a house in Clarksville and stop at a little park. I get out for a few minutes and sit on a bench. I take a couple of long, slow breaths, just letting it all go for a time. It's quiet out here. For a few minutes, nothing moves but the branches of the live oaks in the breeze. Then I take all the money from my pockets and stash it in a canvas bag behind the spare tire. I don't count it. There aren't any scores tonight. But it does look nice in the bag. I get back in the cab and head downtown.

Things finally start to slow down. I've been out ten, eleven hours, but I'm not feeling it yet. After five, I start looking for an excuse to call it a night. It takes awhile, but I finally catch myself yawning. That's it, right there.

When I get home, I pull the canvas bag from the trunk. I've got a bacon cheeseburger and a bag of curly fries. I stand for a minute in the front yard. The city sounds fall away, and I feel the silence gather around me. I watch the sky starting to glow a little in the east, the morning star hanging there, a new day coming up strong. A new year, filled with hope. I take a deep breath, let it out slowly. I feel open and free, ready for whatever it brings.

Then I hear a train horn from down the line, the roar of a faraway diesel heading this way. A dog starts to howl in the distance. I open the door and go inside.

FARTHER DOWN THE ROAD

When I look back at the time I spent as a cabdriver, I realize it was a good time for me. It didn't start out that way, but I was as happy then as I've ever been. And I learned. I learned about the people: the cabdrivers, the passengers, the people on the streets. About the way they lived. And I learned about myself. I learned that I don't have to be pulled along with the highs and lows of everyday life. I learned that setbacks can lead to greater opportunities if I let them. I learned that I can be a better person just by making the effort every day, every moment. I learned to pay attention to what's actually happening, to live now, not in the past and the future. I learned to get over myself, just a little.

And I learned that Dharma Road isn't an asphalt street lined with strip malls and apartment complexes and bars. It leads within. And that's the most important lesson of all.

There's no magic in cabdriving. It's nothing special. It's just a job, a way of getting through the day. There are lessons all around. If you're a doctor, a lawyer, a secret agent, or an Internet billionaire, you can watch the dharma unfold in your own life and follow it wherever it leads. And if you're struggling, down and out, you can make the most of that as well. What else is there to do?

Some time has gone by. More than I'd have thought. I handed in the keys one day, thinking I needed a break, and other things came up. I drove the cab for a few years, and I got out before I got burned out. Someday I might go back, but I don't know when that will be. They say, once a cabdriver, always a cabdriver. Inside, I am.

Things change. The city keeps changing around me. I'll be driving down a road I haven't seen for a while and it looks different. There's another condo project, a parking garage. I have to think about what was there, what's missing now.

The cab business is changing. There aren't as many cab companies now, the drivers can't really move from one to another, playing them off against each other. There's computer dispatching, GPS units, bumper tags for the toll roads they're putting in now. The city is installing red-light cameras at intersections, with an automated system to send out bills for infractions. Automated speed traps are next, I can feel it.

They're taking all the fun out of it. And the adventure. Soon, almost anyone will be able to drive a cab.

It's all right, though. Things change. We just have to deal with that.

Something else has changed. There's a Zen center in Austin, a real sangha. It's been here for a while, but I didn't know about it. I'm not completely on my own with this now. I go there sometimes on Saturday mornings for group zazen, hear a dharma talk that helps put things in perspective. Afterward, I feel my practice renewed, my spirit lifted for a while. I always think I'll spend more time there, learn the sutras they chant, the rituals and ceremonies that everyone but me seems to know. I wish someone would write a book about that. Then maybe I could take a more active role at the center.

But the fact is, that's mostly an excuse. I'm not really a joiner. That hasn't changed.

It's been strange, sitting here at my old Mac, listening to jazz CDs, drinking coffee, writing about the times I had when I was driving the cab. At the time, I felt like I was making the best of a bad situation, but the fact is, I miss it. I liked being out late, working the streets, dealing with whatever came up. I felt free, alive.

I'm still free. And I'm still alive. But I miss it.

Maybe *Dharma Road* will rocket up the bestseller lists, *The Da Vinci Code* for the spiritual set. Maybe it will help people to deal with their day-to-day lives and see beyond that to something deeper and more meaningful. Maybe it will change the world. I hope so. I want to help. And I might make a little money, have a chance to do some things I can't afford to do now. But it won't make as much of a difference in my life as you'd think. No matter what happens, I'll still be me. I'll still have some struggles, a little sadness, and enough of a sense of humor about it all to keep trying.

And I will keep trying. It's what I do.

Sometimes I take a break from writing, make a cup of coffee, and go out on the back porch to let my mind clear. I'll sit out there, listen to the night, watch the bamboo sway in the breeze. I'll watch the cars go by on the ramp that runs up to the Mopac Expressway, a hundred yards or so from the back of the yard. Late at night, I can see the cabs hurrying back to 6th Street looking for that one last fare, the one that makes a winner of the night. And I wish I was out there with them.

And in time, I probably will be.

Well, this is the part where the music starts to play in the background, maybe Lucinda Williams singing "2 kool 2 Be 4-Gotten." The voice-over comes up and ties everything together with a clever little twist. Sorry. No music, no voice-over, no pat ending. No ending at all. Tomorrow we'll all go out and do it again, and maybe we'll be better at it, maybe we'll get a little more out of it. And if we do, that'll be enough.

Here we are. Hope you enjoyed the ride. Watch your step getting out. Have a good one, now.

AIRPORT READING

The cab line at the airport is a great place for cabdrivers to get a little reading done. Sometimes when I get a fare out to the airport, I'll pull into the line to get a break from the traffic and the downtown stress. For an hour or two, I'll just sit out there on a lawn chair or in the front seat of the cab and read about Zen. Sometimes other drivers come by, we'll talk for a while, catch up on the latest rumors, and then I'll go back to my reading. I'm there long enough to do some worthwhile reading, but not so long that it gets to be a chore. Then the lines start moving and I'm on my way again.

If you're heading out to the airport, planning to get in line and do a little reading, here are some titles you might want to consider taking along. All played an important part in the making of *Dharma Road*.

Anger: Wisdom for Cooling the Flames
and anything else by Thich Nhat Hanh

As a young monk, he was nominated for the Nobel Peace Prize by Martin Luther King. Since then, he has written extensively about Buddhism and its role in the modern world. *Living Buddha, Living Christ* also played an important part in Dharma Road, but all of his books are recommended.

The Art of Happiness at Work
and anything else by the Dalai Lama

The Dalai Lama is not only an inspirational spiritual leader. He's also an extremely insightful philosopher with an extensive background in Tibetan Buddhism and many other traditions. He has published numerous books, generally based on his lectures and dialogues. They are all brilliant.

Awakening the Buddha Within:
Tibetan Wisdom for the Western World
by Lama Surya Das

A readable, enjoyable book about the Tibetan practice of Dzogchen by the school's first American lama. He has several other books in print, and all are excellent.

Being Zen
by Ezra Bayda

This book applies Zen practice to real life with an emphasis on dealing with hardships and suffering. If things are going wrong, this book will help. Some of the ideas about dealing with fear and anger expressed in this book came from Bayda. Very inspirational.

Buddha
by Karen Armstrong

The best account of the life and times of the historical Buddha I've seen. It's short, readable, and moving.

Buddhism Is Not What You Think: Finding Freedom Beyond Beliefs
by Steve Hagen

A guide for learning to see through our delusions to our true nature. Very concise and direct. No-nonsense. Hagen once wrote a book titled *Buddhism Without Baloney,* but I haven't seen that.

Buddhism Without Beliefs: A Contemporary Guide to Awakening
by Stephen Batchelor

The author, a longtime Buddhist scholar, demystifies the practice of Buddhism, presenting it as a straightforward plan for a happy and meaningful life without any religious content at all.

The Compass of Zen
by Seung Sahn

A series of talks by the late Korean Zen Master gives an overview of Buddhism, beginning with the most basic concepts of Hinayana Buddhism and building to a dramatic presentation of the most advanced practices of Zen.

The Feeling Buddha
by David Brazier

A thought-provoking reinterpretation of the Buddha's original teachings that presents a more human—and more feeling—version of the dharma.

An Introduction to Haiku
by Harold G. Henderson

I know. There aren't any haikus in *Dharma Road*. There should be. Nothing captures the feel of Zen like haiku. I'm a big fan of Basho. If you can't find this book, any with haikus and some discussion of the form will do.

Kundun
a film by Martin Scorsese

Okay, it's a film, not a book, and you'll have to rent it and watch it at home on a slow night. It's the story of the early life of the Dalai Lama up to his exile from Tibet. It's a great film, and it's by the director of *Taxi Driver*. Make it a double feature.

The Mindful Way through Depression:
Freeing Yourself from Chronic Unhappiness
by Mark Williams, John Teasdale,
Zindel Segal, and Jon Kabat-Zinn

If your Blue Mondays spread into the rest of the week, this book can help. The raisin exercise comes from this.

The Ring of the Way: Testament of a Zen Master
by Taisen Deshimaru

A dramatic series of essays on the philosophy of Soto Zen by a true original. This is probably out of print, but if you can find a copy of anything by Deshimaru, grab it.

The Soul's Religion: Cultivating a Profoundly Spiritual Way of Life
by Thomas Moore

I thought I would hate this book when I checked it out of the library. It looked a little too New Age-y for me. I was wrong. Moore mixes Christianity, Buddhism, and other traditions and makes sense of it all. This and his *Care of the Soul: A Guide for Cultivating Depth and Sacredness in Everyday Life* are highly recommended.

Taking the Path of Zen
by Robert Aitken

This is a clear and concise guide to Zen practice for the beginner. All Robert Aitken's books are beautifully written and accessible. His book about the Ten Grave Precepts, *The Mind of Clover: Essays in Zen Buddhist Ethics*, is another excellent read.

The Tibetan Book of Living and Dying
by Sogyal Rinpoche

Using the *Tibetan Book of the Dead* as a starting point, this book provides a comprehensive view of Tibetan Buddhism with a focus on applying the *Book of the Dead* in life.

Tricycle: The Buddhist Review

This is an excellent magazine providing a wide range of ideas by leading Buddhist scholars. Published bi-monthly. Subscriptions are available. Also check *Buddhism Today* and *Shambhala Sun*.

The Wise Heart: A Guide to the Universal Teachings of Buddhist Psychology
by Jack Kornfield

The author, a psychotherapist and a former Buddhist monk, develops a complete system of transformational psychology based on Buddhist teachings and his own remarkable story.

Zen Driving
by K. T. Berger

The Berger brothers (writing as K. T.) develop a series of ideas relating to Zen practice and driving. Good reading, even for amateur drivers.

Zen in the Art of Archery
by Eugen Herrigel

A classic. The author, who studied in Japan in the 1920s, sets out to learn archery from a Zen master and learns about himself instead. This book first ignited interest in Zen in the West in the 1950s.

Zen Mind, Beginner's Mind
by Shunryu Suzuki

This collection of dharma talks by the founder of the San Francisco Zen Center is the most influential book on Soto Zen practice in the West. It makes the ideas of everyday Zen practice somewhat clear and very enjoyable. A great book.

ABOUT THE AUTHOR

Brian Haycock is a writer and former cab driver residing in Austin, TX. He currently works for a non-profit and secretly misses driving a cab. This is his first book.